Singapore
MATH
CHALLENGE

Terry Chew B.Sc.

GRADE
2+

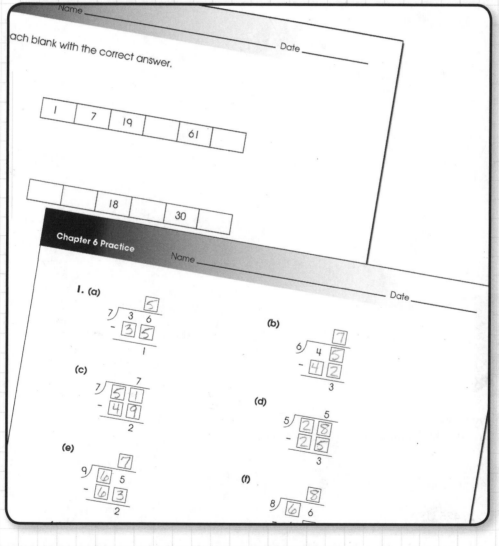

Frank Schaffer Publications®
An imprint of Carson-Dellosa Publishing
Columbus, Ohio

Copyright © Terry Chew
First published in 2008 by Singapore Asia Publishers Pte. Ltd.

Frank Schaffer Publications®
An imprint of Carson-Dellosa Publishing LLC
PO Box 35665
Greensboro, NC 27425 USA

ISBN 978-1-62399-072-5

Letter to Parents..5

Chapter 1 Tell Me the Time! 7

Chapter 2 Intervals...25

Chapter 3 Addition 43

Chapter 4 Solve by Comparison and Replacement............53

Chapter 5 Age Problems...76

Chapter 6 Division 93

Chapter 7 Chicken-and-Rabbit Problems 115

Chapter 8 Looking for a Pattern..132

Chapter 9 Counting...148

Chapter 10 Logic 160

Chapter 11 Make a List, Make a Table......................................175

Chapter 12 Using Models 192

Chapter 13 In Search of a Series...211

Chapter 14 What Comes Next?..232

Chapter 15 Math IQ..245

Chapter 16 Geometry 262

Chapter 17 Odd and Even Numbers...278

Chapter 18 Ordinal Numbers..294

Solutions 311

In *Singapore Math Challenge*, your child will find a variety of intriguing problems and problem-solving methods. Using the step-by-step techniques will help your son or daughter develop skill and creativity as a mathematical thinker.

What is Singapore Math?

Singapore's math curriculum has been recognized worldwide for its excellence in producing students highly skilled in mathematics. Students in Singapore regularly rank at the top of the world in mathematics on the Trends in International Mathematics and Science Study (TIMSS).

The Singapore Math curriculum aims to help students develop necessary concepts and skills for everyday life and to provide students with the ability to formulate, apply, and solve problems. The Singapore Primary (Elementary) Mathematics curriculum covers fewer topics, but in greater depth. Key concepts are introduced and built-on to reinforce mathematical ideas and thinking. Skills are typically taught a full year ahead of when similar skills are taught in the United States.

Singapore Math and the Common Core State Standards

Common Core State Standards in mathematics have been adopted by most U.S. states. These standards are designed to help prepare American students for success in college and in the global twenty-first century workforce. They outline clear, consistent, and rigorous expectations for learning in math.

In developing the Common Core State Standards, experts looked at educationally high-performing nations such as Singapore to identify the best approaches to learning. Singapore math standards are frequently cited in the research used to support the Common Core standards.

Common Core State Standards have raised the bar for American students. Strategies taught in *Singapore Math Challenge* will help students meet these new expectations.

Using *Singapore Math Challenge* Books

Each chapter focuses on a challenging, age-appropriate topic and demonstrates several clever problem-solving methods. Topics in this series include:

- **Basic Concepts:**
  New ways to understand counting, telling time, odd and even numbers, place value, fractions, averaging, and prime numbers

- **Operations:**
  Tricks for solving addition, subtraction, multiplication, and division problems

- **Strategies:**
  Creative and effective approaches to problem solving, including making lists and visual models, making assumptions, comparing and replacing, and working backward

- **Classic Problems:**
  Techniques for solving problems that have interested mathematicians through the ages, including intervals, numbers in a series, speed problems, age problems, and excess-and-shortage problems

- **Logic and IQ:**
  Brain-teasing patterns, puzzles, and logic problems to strengthen mathematical thinking

- **Applied and Advanced Topics:**
  Introductions to squares and cubes, perimeter, area, angles and triangles, percentages, and writing simple algebraic equations

Students should study the examples that begin each chapter and refer back to them often as they attempt to solve the problems. Blank space is provided for working each problem. A complete worked solution for each problem can be found in the back of the book.

Invite your student to think creatively and to try different methods when solving these challenging problems. Above all, encourage your child to approach math endeavors with confidence and to think of math as a fun and fascinating journey.

Tell Me the Time!

Example 1: For each clock, write the correct time on the line provided.

(a)   **(b)**   **(c)**

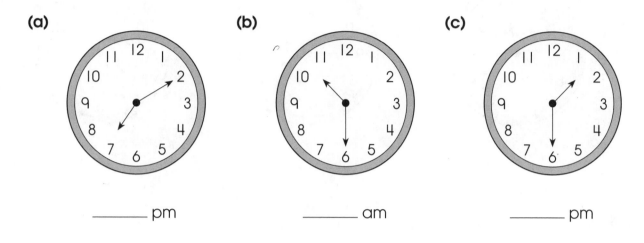

_____ pm   _____ am   _____ pm

Solution:

(a)   7:10

(b)   10:30

(c)   1:30

978-1-62399-072-5
Singapore Math Challenge

Example 2: For each clock, write the correct time on the line provided.

(a)   (b)   (c)

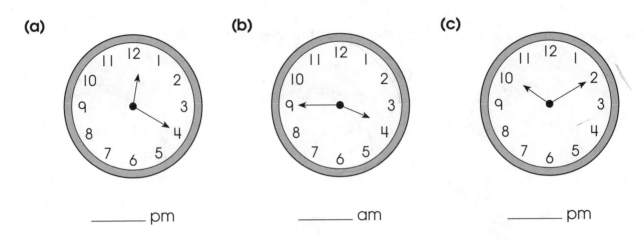

_____ pm   _____ am   _____ pm

Solution:

    (a)   12:20

    (b)   3:45

    (c)   10:10

Example 3: A concert started at 8:30 pm and ended at 10:15 pm. How long did the concert last?

Solution:

From 8:30 pm to 9:30 pm   →   1 hour

From 9:30 pm to 10:30 pm   →   1 hour

1 hour + 1 hour = 2 hours

2 hours − 15 minutes = 1 hour and 45 minutes

The concert lasted 1 hour and 45 minutes.

Example 4: Trains arrive at a subway station every 5 minutes. How many trains would have arrived at the subway station in 30 minutes?

Solution:

1st	2nd	3rd	4th	5th	6th	7th	trains
0	5	10	15	20	25	30	minutes

7 trains would have arrived at the subway station in 30 minutes.

978-1-62399-072-5
Singapore Math Challenge

Example 5: The clocks below are images in a mirror. Write the correct time on the lines provided.

(a)

(b)

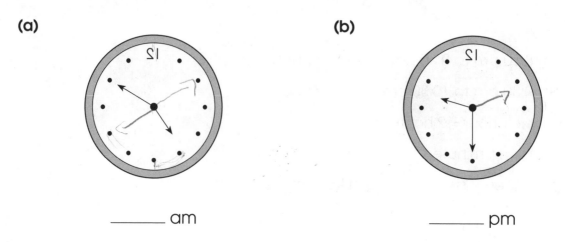

_____ am

_____ pm

Solution:

   (a)   7:10

   (b)   2:30

1. For each clock, write the correct time on the line provided.

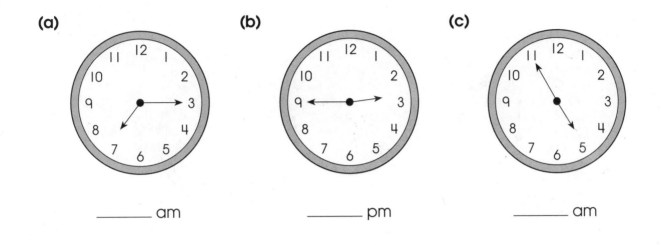

(a)

_____ am

(b)

_____ pm

(c)

_____ am

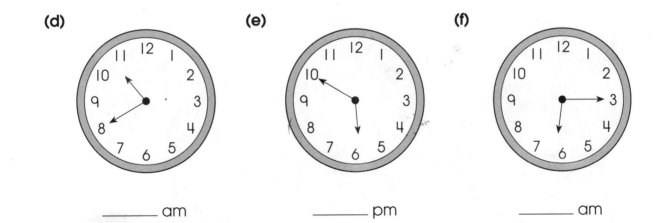

(d)

_____ am

(e)

_____ pm

(f)

_____ am

2. Draw the hour and minute hands on the face of each clock to show the correct time. Write the correct time on the lines provided.

(a) 25 minutes later

2 pm   _____ pm

(b) 40 minutes ago

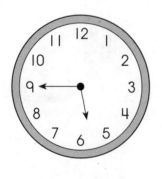

5:45 pm   _____ pm

12   978-1-62399-072-5
Singapore Math Challenge

3. A movie started at 2:30 pm and ended at 4:05 pm. How long was the movie?

978-1-62399-072-5
Singapore Math Challenge

 Name ____________ Date ________

4. The sign shown on the right is placed outside a shop. For how many hours is the shop open daily?

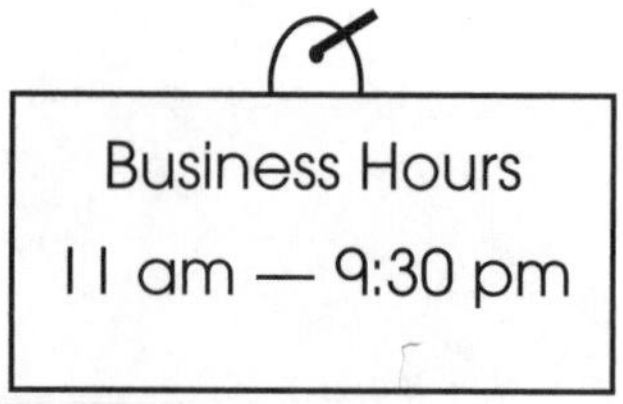
Business Hours
11 am — 9:30 pm

978-1-62399-072-5
Singapore Math Challenge

5. Carl attended a birthday party. The times that the birthday party started and ended are shown on the two clocks below.

starting time   ending time

How long did the birthday party last?

6. Benson played for 10 minutes after reaching home. He watched television for another 20 minutes before eating his lunch. His lunch, which lasted for 20 minutes, was finished at 2:50 pm. At what time did Benson reach home?

7. In the pattern below, draw the hour and minute hands on the face of each clock. Write down the correct time on the lines provided.

7:20 am

8:10 am

8:50 am

_____ am

_____ am

8. Buses arrived at a bus stop every 15 minutes. Lincoln needed to board the bus at 8:30 am but he was late by 8 minutes. At what time did Lincoln arrive at the bus stop? How long did he have to wait for the next bus?

9. The clocks below are images in a mirror. For each clock, write the correct time on the line provided.

(a)

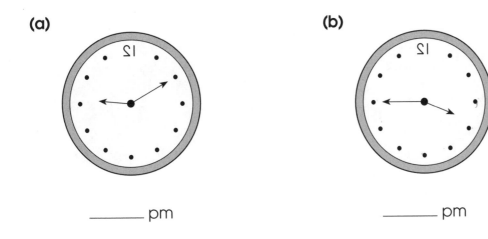

_____ pm

(b)

_____ pm

(c)

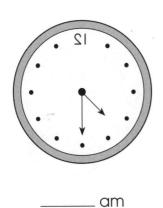

_____ am

(d)

_____ pm

978-1-62399-072-5
Singapore Math Challenge

10. Trains leave a station every 40 minutes. At what time would the third train leave the station if the first train left at 6:30 am?

II. Trains arrive at the subway station every 6 minutes. How many trains would have arrived at the subway station in 60 minutes?

21 978-1-62399-072-5
Singapore Math Challenge

12. Buses leave a station every one and a half hours. If the first bus leaves at five o'clock in the morning, at what time does the fourth bus leave the station?

13. A grandfather clock chimes once at 1 o'clock, twice at 2 o'clock, and three times at 3 o'clock .... How many times would it have chimed by 6 o'clock?

14. The two clocks below show the times Jolene started and ended her birthday party. How long was her birthday party?

starting time   ending time

Intervals

There are many interesting mathematical problems generated from this topic, Intervals.

Example 1: 5 matchsticks are placed at an equal distance away from each other. How many intervals are there?

Solution:

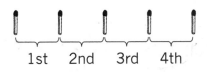

There are 4 intervals.

Example 2: 6 knots are tied on a rope. How many intervals are there from the 1st knot to the 6th knot?

Solution:

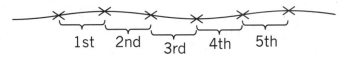

There are 5 intervals.

Example 3: Each staircase has 12 steps. How many steps do 3 such staircases have?

Solution:

3 × 12 = 36

3 such staircases have 36 steps.

Example 4: The road in front of my school is planted with 6 trees. The trees are 4 m away from each other. How far is the sixth tree away from the first one?

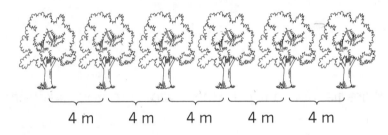

4 m   4 m   4 m   4 m   4 m

Solution:

5 × 4 m = 20 m

The sixth tree is 20 m away from the first one.

Example 5: The distance between the first and the eighth trees along a stretch of road is 21 m. How far are the trees away from each other along that stretch of road if they are placed at regular intervals?

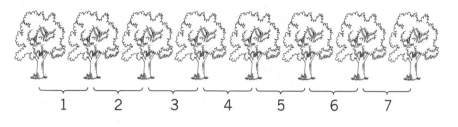

Solution:

$$21 \text{ m} \div 7 = 3 \text{ m}$$

The trees are 3 m away from each other along that stretch of road.

978-1-62399-072-5
Singapore Math Challenge

1. 8 trees are planted at the same distance away from each other along a stretch of road. How many intervals are there?

2. There are 8 lamp posts along a stretch of road. In between every 2 lamp posts, there are 2 trees. How many trees are there along that stretch of road?

3. There are 4 trees along the road in front of Edward's house. The trees are 3 m away from each other. How far is the fourth tree from the first one?

4. There are 5 lamp posts along the street in front of Melissa's house. The lamp posts are 5 m apart from each other. How far is the fourth lamp post from the first one?

978-1-62399-072-5
Singapore Math Challenge

5. Jimmy ties 5 knots on a piece of rope. The knots are 20 cm apart from one another. How far is the fifth knot from the first one?

6. 7 trees are planted along a stretch of road. The distance between every two trees is 3 m. How far is the sixth tree from the second one?

© Singapore Asia Publishers Pte Ltd   978-1-62399-072-5
Singapore Math Challenge

7. Stella lines up 9 coins on a table. Each coin is 10 cm apart. How far is the ninth coin from the first one?

8. It takes Peter 5 minutes to saw a plank of wood into two pieces. How many minutes will Peter take to saw a plank of the same length into four pieces?

9. A grandfather clock takes 6 seconds to chime 4 times at 4 o'clock. How many seconds will the grandfather clock take to chime 6 times at 6 o'clock?

978-1-62399-072-5
Singapore Math Challenge

10. Alison lives on the 5th floor of an apartment building. The staircase leading to each floor has 10 steps. How many steps does Alison have to climb before she reaches home?

11. A subway train takes 2 minutes to reach the next station. It stays at a station for 1 minute before moving to the next station. How many minutes does the subway train take to travel from the first to the fifth station?

12. A train has 6 compartments. Each compartment is 6 m long. The compartments are joined by connectors that are 1 m in length. How long is the train?

13. Buses leave a station every 10 minutes. How many buses would have left the station in 60 minutes?

14. To make 8 equal pieces, how many times do you need to cut a ribbon that is 80 cm long? How long is each piece of ribbon?

978-1-62399-072-5
Singapore Math Challenge

15. Vanessa uses some coins to form a triangle. Each of the 3 corners of the triangle has a coin. There are 5 coins on each side of the triangle. How many coins does Vanessa use to form the triangle?

Addition

(A) <u>Making tens and hundreds</u>

Example 1: Add the numbers below by making a ten.

(a)
$$3 + 5 + 7$$
$$= 10 + 5$$
$$= 15$$

(b)
$$4 + 7 + 6$$
$$= 10 + 7$$
$$= 17$$

(c)
$$5 + 4 + 5$$
$$= 10 + 4$$
$$= 14$$

(d)
$$2 + 9 + 8$$
$$= 10 + 9$$
$$= 19$$

(e)
$$4 + 5 + 6 + 5$$
$$= 10 + 10$$
$$= 20$$

(f)
$$7 + 8 + 2 + 3$$
$$= 10 + 10$$
$$= 20$$

978-1-62399-072-5
Singapore Math Challenge

Example 2: Add the numbers by making tens or hundreds.

(a) $\overparen{35 + 15}\ 100 + 65$
= 100 + 15
= 115

(b) $\overparen{45 + 55}\ 100 + 20$
= 100 + 20
= 120

(c) $\overparen{38 + 22}\ 60 + 16$
= 60 + 16
= 76

(d) $\overparen{42 + 16 + 38}\ 80$
= 80 + 16
= 96

(e) $15 + \overparen{32 + 48}\ 80 + 5$
$\underparen{15 + \ \ \ \ \ \ \ \ \ + 5}\ 20$
= 80 + 20
= 100

(f) $\overparen{17 + 13}\ 30 + \overparen{25 + 35}\ 60$
= 30 + 60
= 90

(B) <u>Breaking up or rounding up numbers</u>

Example 1: Find the value of 17 + 18 + 19.

17 + 18 + 19 = 20 − 3 + 20 − 2 + 20 − 1
= 60 − 3 − 2 − 1
= 60 − 6
= 54

Example 2: Find the value of 37 + 38 + 35.

$$37 + 38 + 35 = 30 + 7 + 30 + 8 + 30 + 5$$
$$= 90 + 7 + 8 + 5$$
$$= 90 + 7 + 8 + 3 + 2$$
$$= 90 + 20$$
$$= 110$$

Example 3: Find the value of 17 + 21 + 14.

$$17 + 21 + 14 = 17 + 3 + 11 + 21$$
$$= 20 + 32$$
$$= 52$$

Example 4: Find the value of 9 + 99 + 999.

$$9 + 99 + 999 = 10 - 1 + 100 - 1 + 1{,}000 - 1$$
$$= 1{,}000 + 100 + 10 - 3$$
$$= 1{,}110 - 3$$
$$= 1{,}107$$

978-1-62399-072-5
Singapore Math Challenge

(C) <u>Express a number as a sum of 2 or 3 numbers</u>

Example 1:

$$2 \quad 3 \quad 5 \quad 7 \quad 11 \quad 13 \quad 17 \quad 19 \quad 23 \quad 29$$

Express each number below as the sum of 2 numbers given above.

(a) $10 = 7 + 3$

(b) $12 = 7 + 5$

(c) $18 = 5 + 13$
      or
   $18 = 7 + 11$

(d) $30 = 11 + 19$
       or
   $30 = 13 + 17$
       or
   $30 = 23 + 7$

Example 2:

$$2 \quad 3 \quad 5 \quad 7 \quad 11 \quad 13 \quad 17 \quad 19 \quad 23 \quad 29 \quad 31 \quad 33$$

Express each number below as the sum of 3 numbers given above.

(a) $10 = 2 + 3 + 5$

(b) $24 = 2 + 3 + 19$
        or
   $24 = 2 + 5 + 17$

(c) $46 = 2 + 13 + 31$
        or
   $46 = 2 + 11 + 33$

(d) $39 = 3 + 7 + 29$
        or
   $39 = 3 + 17 + 19$

978-1-62399-072-5
Singapore Math Challenge

1. Add the numbers by making tens.

(a) $2 + 8 + 3 + 7$

(b) $5 + 4 + 6 + 5$

(c) $9 + 2 + 8 + 1$

(d) $14 + 16 + 21 + 29$

(e) $13 + 28 + 22 + 17$

(f) $15 + 37 + 23 + 25$

(g) $26 + 14 + 33 + 37$

(h) $18 + 19 + 22 + 11$

(i) $28 + 32 + 15 + 25$

(j) $32 + 22 + 28 + 10$

(k) $42 + 16 + 15 + 18$

(l) $18 + 13 + 22 + 28$

2. Find the values of the following.

(a) $9 + 8 + 10$

(b) $7 + 8 + 9$

(c) $7 + 8 + 9 + 11$

(d) $10 + 19 + 17$

(e) $18 + 19 + 20$

(f) $9 + 19 + 39$

(g) $18 + 28 + 38$

(h) $16 + 17 + 18 + 19$

3. Find the values of the following.

    (a) $18 + 19 + 13$

    (b) $17 + 18 + 15$

    (c) $21 + 22 + 23 + 24$

    (d) $19 + 17 + 14 + 21$

    (e) $33 + 24 + 13 + 14$

    (f) $28 + 23 + 9 + 22$

    (g) $29 + 23 + 28 + 16$

    (h) $27 + 4 + 29 + 35$

4. 2   3   5   7   11   13   17   19   23   29

Express each number below as the sum of 2 numbers given above.

(a) 7 = (   ) + (   )

(b) 12 = (   ) + (   )

(c) 18 = (   ) + (   )

     18 = (   ) + (   )

(d) 36 = (   ) + (   )

     36 = (   ) + (   )

     36 = (   ) + (   )

(e) 42 = (   ) + (   )

     42 = (   ) + (   )

(f) 48 = (   ) + (   )

978-1-62399-072-5
Singapore Math Challenge

5. Express each number as the sum of 3 numbers given in question 4.

(a) $10 = (\quad) + (\quad) + (\quad)$

(b) $23 = (\quad) + (\quad) + (\quad) = (\quad) + (\quad) + (\quad)$

(c) $38 = (\quad) + (\quad) + (\quad) = (\quad) + (\quad) + (\quad)$

(d) $37 = (\quad) + (\quad) + (\quad) = (\quad) + (\quad) + (\quad)$

(e) $41 = (\quad) + (\quad) + (\quad) = (\quad) + (\quad) + (\quad)$

(f) $49 = (\quad) + (\quad) + (\quad) = (\quad) + (\quad) + (\quad)$

978-1-62399-072-5
Singapore Math Challenge

6. Fill in each box with the correct answer to make the addition work.

(a)

```
   □   3
+  3   □
─────────
   5   8
```

(b)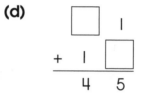

```
   2   □
+  □   5
─────────
   7   2
```

(c)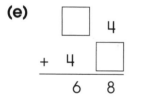

```
   I   □
+  □   I
─────────
   3   9
```

(d)

```
   □   I
+  I   □
─────────
   4   5
```

(e)

```
   □   4
+  4   □
─────────
   6   8
```

(f)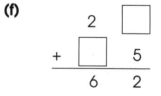

```
   2   □
+  □   5
─────────
   6   2
```

(g)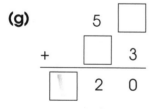

```
      5   □
+     □   3
─────────────
   □  2   0
```

(h)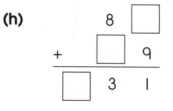

```
      8   □
+     □   9
─────────────
   □  3   I
```

978-1-62399-072-5
Singapore Math Challenge

Solve by Comparison and Replacement

Example 1:

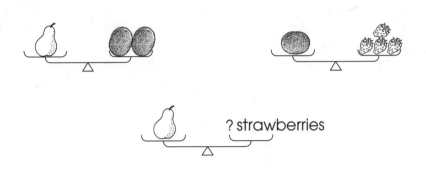

? strawberries

Solution:

By comparison,

1 pear　　　→ 2 kiwi fruit

1 kiwi fruit → 4 strawberries

2 kiwi fruit → 8 strawberries

1 pear　　　→ 8 strawberries

978-1-62399-072-5
Singapore Math Challenge

Example 2:

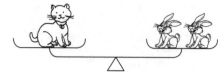 

? chicks

Solution:

By comparison,

1 cat   → 2 rabbits

3 cats   → 6 rabbits

3 rabbits → 4 chicks

6 rabbits → 8 chicks

3 cats   → 8 chicks

Example 3: $\triangle + \bigcirc = 13$
$\triangle - \bigcirc = 3$
$\triangle = ?$ $\bigcirc = ?$

Solution:

We may add up the two statements.

$\triangle + \triangle + \bigcirc - \bigcirc = 13 + 3$

$\triangle + \triangle = 16$

$\triangle = 16 \div 2 = 8$ $\bigcirc = 13 - 8 = 5$

Example 4: $\square + \bigcirc = 15$
$\square + \square + \bigcirc + \bigcirc + \bigcirc = 35$

Solution:

We may rearrange the second statement.

$\square + \square + \bigcirc + \bigcirc + \bigcirc = 35$

$\underbrace{\square + \bigcirc}_{15} + \underbrace{\square + \bigcirc}_{15} + \bigcirc = 35$

$30 + \bigcirc = 35$

$\bigcirc = 35 - 30 = 5$ $\square = 15 - 5 = 10$

1.

? eggs

2.

? chicks

3.

$$\bigcirc + \square = 14$$
$$\bigcirc - \square = 6$$

$$\bigcirc = ?\quad \square = ?$$

10   4

4.

$$\square + \triangle = 15$$
$$\triangle - \square = 7$$

$$\triangle = ? \qquad \square = ?$$

5.

$$* - \square = 22$$
$$* + \square = 30$$

$$* = ?   \square = ?$$

6.

$$❖ + ✳ + ❖ = 15$$
$$✳ + ❖ = 11$$

$$❖ = ? \qquad ✳ = ?$$

7.

$$\bigcirc + \bigcirc + \bigcirc + ✳ = 22$$
$$\bigcirc + ✳ = 12$$

$$\bigcirc = ? \qquad ✳ = ?$$

8.

$$❖ + ✳ + ✳ = 14$$
$$❖ + ❖ + ❖ + ✳ + ✳ = 18$$

$$❖ = ? \qquad ✳ = ?$$

978-1-62399-072-5
Singapore Math Challenge

9.

$$\square + \bigcirc + \bigcirc = 14$$
$$\square + \bigcirc + \bigcirc + \bigcirc + \bigcirc = 24$$

$$\square = ? \qquad\qquad \bigcirc = ?$$

978-1-62399-072-5
Singapore Math Challenge

10.

? apples

11.

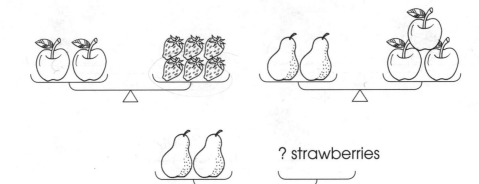

? strawberries

12.

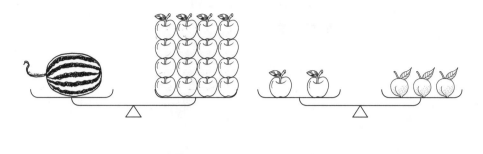

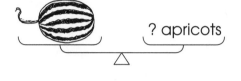

? apricots

13.

$$* + ❖ = 22$$
$$* + * + ❖ + ❖ + ❖ = 58$$

$$* = ?$$ $$❖ = ?$$

14.

$$* + \bigcirc = 25$$
$$* + * + * + \bigcirc + \bigcirc = 65$$

$$* = ? \qquad \bigcirc = ?$$

15.

$$❖ + ◯ = 9$$
$$◯ + ☐ = 12$$
$$☐ + ❖ = 11$$

$$❖ = ?\qquad ☐ = ?\qquad ◯ = ?$$

16.
$$❖ + \Delta + \Delta + \Delta + \Delta = 33$$
$$❖ + ❖ = \Delta + \Delta + \Delta$$

$$❖ = ? \qquad\qquad \Delta = ?$$

17.

$$\bigcirc \times \ast = 24$$
$$\bigcirc + \ast = 11$$
$$\bigcirc + \ast + \Delta = 17$$

$$\Delta = ?$$

978-1-62399-072-5
Singapore Math Challenge

19.

$$* \times \bigcirc = 24$$
$$\bigcirc \times \square = 40$$
$$\square \times \diamondsuit = 45$$
$$* \times \square = 15$$

$$* = ? \quad \bigcirc = ? \quad \diamondsuit = ? \quad \square = ?$$

18.

$$\Diamond \times \bigcirc = \clubsuit$$
$$\Diamond + \Diamond + \Diamond = \clubsuit - \Diamond$$

$$\bigcirc = ?$$

20.

$$\diamond \times \bigcirc = 30$$
$$* \times \diamond = 12$$
$$* \times \bigcirc = 10$$

$* = ?$ $\diamond = ?$ $\bigcirc = ?$

Age Problems

Remember the two points below when working on age problems.

I. The difference in age between two people will remain the same.

2. The multiple of a person's age to another age will change with time.

Example I: Amanda is 7 years old.
Her father is 36 years old.
How many years older will her father be than Amanda in 4 years' time?

Solution:

The difference in age between them will remain the same.

$$36 - 7 = 29$$

Her father will be 29 years older than Amanda in 4 years' time.

Example 2: Mr. Jensen is 45 years old.
His daughter, Natalie, is 8 years old.
How many years older will Mr. Jensen be than Natalie in 5 years' time?

Solution:

The difference in age between them will remain the same.

$$45 - 8 = 37$$

Mr. Jensen will be 37 years older than Natalie in 5 years' time.

Example 3: Andrew is 8 years old.
His mother is 32 years old.
How many times Andrew's age is his mother's age?

Solution:

$$4 \times 8 = 32$$
$$\text{or}$$
$$32 \div 8 = 4$$

His mother is 4 times as old as Andrew.

Example 4: Paula is 6 years old.
Her father will be 40 years old when Paula reaches the age of 10. How old is Paula's father?

Solution:

$$10 - 6 = 4$$
$$40 - 4 = 36$$

Paula's father is 36 years old.

Example 5: Edward is 8 years old.

His mother is 32 years old.

In how many years' time will his mother be 3 times as old as Edward?

Solution:

Since the difference in age will remain the same, we can make a table as shown on the right.

$36 \div 12 = 3$

$12 - 8 = 4$

or

$36 - 32 = 4$

Edward's age	His mother's age
8	32
9	33
10	34
11	35
12	36

His mother will be 3 times as old as Edward in 4 years' time.

978-1-62399-072-5
Singapore Math Challenge

1. My mother is 25 years younger than my grandmother.
How many years older was my grandmother than my mother 5 years ago?

2. Chloe is 4 years old.
Her father is 36 years old.
How many years younger will Chloe be than her father in 8 years' time?

3. Shelia's father is 35 years old.
Her grandfather is 62 years old.
How old will each of them be in 12 years' time?

4. Tom is 6 years old.
His brother is 11 years old.
How many years older than Tom is his brother?
How many years younger will Tom be than his brother in 10 years' time?

5. The sum of Valerie's, her sister's and their father's ages is 85.
Valerie is 22 years old. She is twice as old as her sister.
How old is their father?

6. My granny is 56 years old.
   My mother is 31 years old.
   I am 7 years old.
   In how many years' time will the sum of our ages be 100?

         978-1-62399-072-5

7. Wilfred is 4 years old.
His father's age is 7 times his age.
How old is his father?

85

978-1-62399-072-5
Singapore Math Challenge

8. When Teddy was 5 years old, his father's age was 7 times Teddy's age. When his father is 40 years old, how old will Teddy be?

9. Julia's mother is 36 years old.
Her father is 42 years old.
Given that Julia is 7 years old, in how many years' time will the sum of all their ages be 100?

10. Phyllis is 5 years old.
Her father is 40 years old.
In how many years' time will her father's age be 6 times Phyllis's age?

978-1-62399-072-5
Singapore Math Challenge

11. Anna is 5 years old.
Her mother is 33 years old.
In how many years' time will her mother's age be 5 times her age?

978-1-62399-072-5
Singapore Math Challenge

12. Wendy is 6 years old.
The sum of her age and her sister's age will be 40 in 9 years' time.
How old is Wendy's sister?

90

13. Mr. Gibson is 5 years older than Mrs. Gibson.
The sum of their ages will be 95 in 5 years' time.
How old is each?

14. Mrs. Woody is 38 years old. She is 4 years younger than Mr. Woody.
Jim, their youngest son, is 8 years old.
How many years from now will the sum of all their ages be 100?

Division

Recall the multiplication tables.

$$4 \times 8 = 32$$

We can write a division statement based on the above multiplication sentence. The terms used in division are listed below.

$$\underset{\text{(dividend)}}{32} \quad \underset{}{\div} \quad \underset{\text{(divisor)}}{4} \quad = \quad \underset{\text{(quotient)}}{8}$$

In the case of remainders, we may write them in the following way.

$$35 \div 4 = 8 \text{ R } 3$$

This means that $4 \times 8 + 3 = 35$.

Important note: The remainder must be smaller than the divisor.

978-1-62399-072-5
Singapore Math Challenge

Example 1: Fill in each box with the correct answer to make the division work.

(a)

(b)

Solution:

(a)   Recall the multiplication table.

$9 \times 5 = 45$

$48 - 45 = 3$

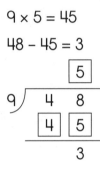

(b) $7 \times 5 = 35$

$35 + 6 = 41$

Example 2: Find all the possible dividends where the quotients and the remainders are the same.

$$\boxed{} \div 5 = \boxed{} R \boxed{}$$

Solution:

1st answer: $\boxed{24} \div 5 = \boxed{4} R \boxed{4}$

$5 \times 4 = 20$

$20 + 4 = 24$

2nd answer: $\boxed{18} \div 5 = \boxed{3} R \boxed{3}$

$5 \times 3 = 15$

$15 + 3 = 18$

3rd answer: $\boxed{12} \div 5 = \boxed{2} R \boxed{2}$

$5 \times 2 = 10$

$10 + 2 = 12$

4th answer: $\boxed{6} \div 5 = \boxed{1} R \boxed{1}$

$5 \times 1 = 5$

$5 + 1 = 6$

Example 3: Fill in each box with the correct answer.

$$25 \div \boxed{} = \boxed{} \text{R } 1$$

Solution:

$6 \times 4 = 4 \times 6 = 24$

$24 + 1 = 25$

$25 \div \boxed{4} = \boxed{6} \text{R } 1$ or $25 \div \boxed{6} = \boxed{4} \text{R } 1$

978-1-62399-072-5
Singapore Math Challenge

Example 4: Some black and white beads are arranged in the following manner.

○○●●●○○●●●○○●●● ⋯

What is the color of the 24th bead?
What is the color of the 32nd bead?

Solution:

This pattern repeats after every 5 beads.

$24 \div 5 = 4 \text{ R } 4$

○　　○　　●　　●　　●

R1　R2　R3　R4　R0

The color of the 24th bead is black.

$32 \div 5 = 6 \text{ R } 2$

The color of the 32nd bead is white.

Example 5: Some years ago, March 1ˢᵗ was a Sunday.
Which day of the week was March 25ᵗʰ that year?

Solution:

Method 1: Draw a Table

Sun.	Mon.	Tue.	Wed.	Thur.	Fri.	Sat.
1	2	3	4	5	6	7
8	9	10	11	12	13	14
15	16	17	18	19	20	21
22	23	24	25	...	...	...

Method 2: Solve by Reasoning

There are 7 days in a week.

$25 \div 7 = 3 \text{ R } 4$

Sun.	Mon.	Tue.	Wed.	Thur.	Fri.	Sat.
R1	R2	R3	R4	R5	R6	R0

March 25ᵗʰ was a Wednesday that year.

1. (a)

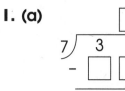

(b)

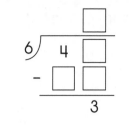

(c)

(d)

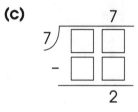

(e)

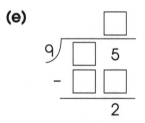

(f)

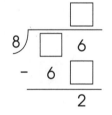

(g)

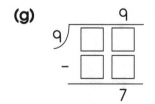

(h)

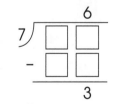

978-1-62399-072-5
Singapore Math Challenge

2. Fill in each box with a correct single-digit answer.

(a) $26 \div \boxed{} = \boxed{} \text{R } 2$

(b) $39 \div \boxed{} = \boxed{} \text{R } 3$

(c) $47 \div \boxed{} = \boxed{} \text{R } 2$

(d) $58 \div \boxed{} = \boxed{} \text{R } 4$

(e) $68 \div \boxed{} = \boxed{} \text{R } 5$

(f) $78 \div \boxed{} = \boxed{} \text{R } 6$

978-1-62399-072-5
Singapore Math Challenge

3. Fill in each box with the correct answer where the remainder is the smallest.

(a) ☐ ÷ 6 = 5 R ☐

(b) ☐ ÷ 7 = 7 R ☐

(c) ☐ ÷ 8 = 7 R ☐

(d) ☐ ÷ 9 = 7 R ☐

4. Fill in each box with the correct answer where the remainder is the greatest. The greatest remainder should be smaller than the divisor.

(a) ☐ ÷ 3 = 5 R ☐

(b) ☐ ÷ 5 = 7 R ☐

(c) ☐ ÷ 4 = 6 R ☐

(d) ☐ ÷ 6 = 5 R ☐

(e) ☐ ÷ 6 = 7 R ☐

(f) ☐ ÷ 7 = 8 R ☐

978-1-62399-072-5
Singapore Math Challenge

5. Fill in each box with the correct answer where the divisor is the smallest. The divisor should be greater than the remainder.

(a) $\boxed{} \div \boxed{} = 5 \text{ R } 4$

(b) $\boxed{} \div \boxed{} = 7 \text{ R } 3$

(c) $\boxed{} \div \boxed{} = 6 \text{ R } 5$

(d) $\boxed{} \div \boxed{} = 8 \text{ R } 4$

(e) $\boxed{} \div \boxed{} = 9 \text{ R } 3$

(f) $\boxed{} \div \boxed{} = 9 \text{ R } 5$

6. Fill in each box with the correct answer so that the quotient and the remainder must have the same value.

$$\square \div 6 = \square \ R \ \square$$

$$\square \div 6 = \square \ R \ \square$$

$$\square \div 6 = \square \ R \ \square$$

$$\square \div 6 = \square \ R \ \square$$

$$\square \div 6 = \square \ R \ \square$$

978-1-62399-072-5
Singapore Math Challenge

7. Some gray and white beads are arranged in the following pattern.

○ ● ● ○ ● ● ○ ● ● ...

What is the color of the 23rd bead?
What is the color of the 31st bead?

8. Look at the pattern below.

○ ○ □ □ □ ○ ○ □ □ □ ○ ○ □ □ □ ⋯

What is the shape of the 26ᵗʰ figure in the above pattern?
What is the shape of the 33ʳᵈ figure in the above pattern?

9. 34 number cards are given out to Charmaine, Shola and Amy in this manner.

Charmaine	Shola	Amy
1	2	3
4	5	6
...	...	...
...	...	...

Who will get the last card?

978-1-62399-072-5
Singapore Math Challenge

10. 54 marbles are shared among Jolene, Anna and Jim in this manner.

Jolene	Anna	Jim
1	2	1
1	2	1
...	...	...
...	...	...

Who will get the last marble?

978-1-62399-072-5
Singapore Math Challenge

11. A string of numbers is arranged in the following pattern.

1, 3, 2, 4, 1, 3, 2, 4, 1, 3, 2, 4, ...

What is the 27th number?

What is the 42nd number?

12. Some lanterns are hung in the following pattern: 3 red lanterns; 2 orange lanterns; 1 pink lantern; 3 red lanterns; 2 orange lanterns; 1 pink lantern; ....
What is the color of the 38th lantern?
What is the color of the 58th lantern?

978-1-62399-072-5
Singapore Math Challenge

13. Some years ago, May 1st was a Wednesday.
   Which day of the week was May 23rd that year?

Method 1: Solve by Reasoning

Method 2: Draw a Table

Sun.	Mon.	Tue.	Wed.	Thur.	Fri.	Sat.

14. Some years ago, March 20ᵗʰ fell on a Sunday.
Which day of the week was April 11ᵗʰ that year?

Method 1: Solve by Reasoning

Method 2: Draw a Table

Sun.	Mon.	Tue.	Wed.	Thur.	Fri.	Sat.

15. A 2-digit number has a remainder of 1 when it is divided by 3. It also has a remainder of 1 when it is divided by 5.

What is the 2-digit number?

978-1-62399-072-5

Singapore Math Challenge

16. A 2-digit number has a remainder of 2 when it is divided by 4. It also has a remainder of 2 when it is divided by 5.
Find the 2-digit number.

978-1-62399-072-5
Singapore Math Challenge

Chicken-and-Rabbit Problems

Example 1: 4 chickens and rabbits have 10 legs altogether. How many chickens are there? How many rabbits are there?

Solution:

Method 1: Solve by Drawing

Step 1:   We draw 4 ovals to represent the chickens and rabbits.

Step 2:   Assume all were chickens,

$2 \times 4 = 8$

$10 - 8 = 2$

2 more legs are needed to add on.

Step 3:

There are 3 chickens and 1 rabbit.

978-1-62399-072-5
Singapore Math Challenge

Method 2: Make a Table

Step 1:   We shall begin with 2 chickens and 2 rabbits.

No. of chickens	No. of legs	No. of rabbits	No. of legs	Total no. of legs
2	2 × 2 = 4	2	2 × 4 = 8	4 + 8 = 12

Step 2:   Decrease the number of rabbits by 1. At the same time, increase the number of chickens by 1.

No. of chickens	No. of legs	No. of rabbits	No. of legs	Total no. of legs
2	2 × 2 = 4	2	2 × 4 = 8	4 + 8 = 12
3	3 × 2 = 6	1	1 × 4 = 4	6 + 4 = 10

There are 3 chickens and 1 rabbit.

Example 2: A spider has 8 legs.
A dragonfly has 6 legs.
6 spiders and dragonflies have 40 legs altogether.
How many spiders are there?
How many dragonflies are there?

Solution:

Method 1: Solve by Drawing

Step 1: We make 6 ovals to represent the insects.

Step 2: Assume all were dragonflies,

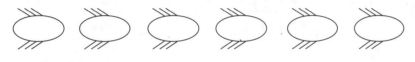

6 × 6 = 36

40 − 36 = 4

4 more legs are needed to add on.

Step 3:

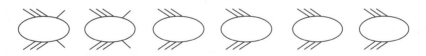

There are 2 spiders and 4 dragonflies.

Method 2: Make a Table

Step 1:   We shall begin with 3 spiders and 3 dragonflies.

No. of spiders	No. of legs	No. of dragonflies	No. of legs	Total no. of legs
3	3 × 8 = 24	3	3 × 6 = 18	24 + 18 = 42

Step 2:   42 − 40 = 2

Decrease the number of spiders by 1. At the same time, increase the number of dragonflies by 1.

No. of spiders	No. of legs	No. of dragonflies	No. of legs	Total no. of legs
3	3 × 8 = 24	3	3 × 6 = 18	24 + 18 = 42
2	2 × 8 = 16	4	4 × 6 = 24	16 + 24 = 40

There are 2 spiders and 4 dragonflies.

978-1-62399-072-5
Singapore Math Challenge

Example 3: A pencil cost $2. A pen cost $4. David paid $20 for 6 such pens and pencils. How many pens did he buy? How many pencils did he buy?

Solution:

Method 1: Solve by Drawing

Step 1:   If all were pencils,

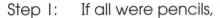

$6 \times \$2 = \$12$

$\$20 - \$12 = \$8$

$8 more are needed to add on.

Step 2:

He bought 4 pens and 2 pencils.

Method 2: Make a Table

No. of pens	Value	No. of pencils	Value	Total value
3	$3 \times \$4 = \$12$	3	$3 \times \$2 = \$6$	$\$12 + \$6 = \$18$
4	$4 \times \$4 = \$16$	2	$2 \times \$2 = \$4$	$\$16 + \$4 = \$20$

He bought 4 pens and 2 pencils.

As the numbers get bigger, it becomes tedious to use methods 1 or 2. We shall now introduce the third method to solve problems of this nature.

Example 4: A farmer has 11 chickens and rabbits. These animals have a total of 30 legs.
How many chickens does he have?
How many rabbits does he have?

Solution:

Method 3: Solve by Assuming

Step 1:   If all were chickens,

$11 \times 2 = 22$

$30 - 22 = 8$

why was there a shortage of 8 legs?

<u>Some</u> rabbits were counted as chickens.

Step 2:   A chicken has 2 legs.

A rabbit has 4 legs.

The difference in the number of legs is

$4 - 2 = 2$.

Step 3: $8 \div 2 = 4$ rabbits

$11 - 4 = 7$ chickens

He has 4 rabbits and 7 chickens.

Example 5: Andrea paid $45 in all for twelve books.
How many 2-dollar books did she buy?
How many 5-dollar books did she buy?

Solution:

Method 3: Solve by Assuming

Step 1:   If all were 2-dollar books,

$12 \times \$2 = \$24$

$\$45 - \$24 = \$21$

there was a shortage of $21 as some books were 5-dollar books.

Step 2: $\$5 - \$2 = \$3$

The difference in value between the two types of books is $3.

Step 3: $\$21 \div \$3 = $ seven 5-dollar books

$12 - 7 = $ five 2-dollar books

She bought seven 5-dollar books and five 2-dollar books.

I. There are 8 cars and motorcycles in a parking lot. There are a total of 26 wheels.
How many cars are in the parking lot?
How many motorcycles are in the parking lot?

Method I: **Solve by Drawing**

Method 2: **Make a Table**

No. of cars	No. of wheels	No. of motorcycles	No. of wheels	Total no. of wheels

2. An adult movie ticket cost $8.
A child movie ticket cost $5.
Mr. Fox paid $31 in all for 5 movie tickets.
How many adult movie tickets did he buy?
How many child movie tickets did he buy?

x = adult
y = child

2 adult
3 child

Method 1: Solve by Drawing

$8x + y = 81$
$8f + y = 40$

$8x + 8y = 40$
$8x + 5y =$

$3y = 9$
$3 \quad 3$
$y = 3$

Method 2: Make a Table

No. of adult movie tickets	Value	No. of child movie tickets	Value	Total value

978-1-62399-072-5
Singapore Math Challenge

3. A science fiction book cost $5.
   A book on adventures cost $3.
   Louisa paid $26 in all for 6 books.
   How many science fiction books did she buy?
   How many books on adventures did she buy?

Method I: Solve by Drawing

Method 2: Make a Table

No. of science fiction books	Value	No. of books on adventures	Value	Total value

4. A tricycle has 3 wheels.
A bicycle has 2 wheels.
8 tricycles and bicycles have 22 wheels altogether.
How many tricycles are there?
How many bicycles are there?

Method 1: Solve by Drawing

Method 2: Make a Table

No. of bicycles	No. of wheels	No. of tricycles	No. of wheels	Total no. of wheels

5. A farmer has 12 chickens and rabbits.
There are 34 legs altogether.
How many chickens does the farmer have?
How many rabbits does the farmer have?

Method 1: Solve by Drawing

Method 2: Make a Table

No. of chickens	No. of legs	No. of rabbits	No. of legs	Total no. of legs

978-1-62399-072-5
Singapore Math Challenge

6. A farmer has 17 chickens and rabbits.
She counts 52 legs in all.
How many chickens does she have?
How many rabbits does she have?

Method 1: Make a Table

No. of chickens	No. of legs	No. of rabbits	No. of legs	Total no. of legs

Method 2: Solve by Assuming

7. A big box can hold 12 marbles.
A small box can hold 6 marbles.
84 marbles are to be placed into 10 boxes.
How many big boxes are there?
How many small boxes are there?

Method 1: Make a Table

No. of big boxes	No. of marbles	No. of small boxes	No. of marbles	Total no. of marbles

Method 2: Solve by Assuming

8. A spider has 8 legs.
A dragonfly has 6 legs.
10 spiders and dragonflies have 68 legs altogether.
How many spiders are there?
How many dragonflies are there?

Method 1: Solve by Drawing

Method 2: Solve by Assuming

9. Randy paid $16 in all for 11 postcards.
How many two-dollar postcards did he buy?
How many one-dollar postcards did he buy?

Method 1: Solve by Drawing

Method 2: Solve by Assuming

10. A truck has 6 wheels.
A car has 4 wheels.
14 trucks and cars parked in a parking lot have a total of 72 wheels.
How many trucks are there?
How many cars are there?

Method 1: Make a Table

No. of trucks	No. of wheels	No. of cars	No. of wheels	Total no. of wheels

Method 2: Solve by Assuming

Looking for a Pattern

Example 1: Complete the number patterns.

(a) 1, 3, 5, 7, (   ), (   ), ...
(b) 2, 3, 5, 8, (   ), (   ), ...
(c) 1, 4, 9, 16, (   ), (   ), ...
(d) 2, 5, 11, 23, (   ), (   ), ...

Solution:

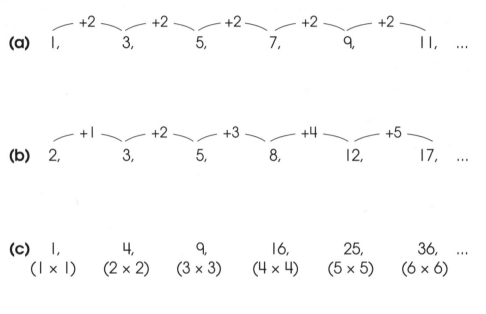

(a) 1, 3, 5, 7, 9, 11, ... (each +2)

(b) 2, 3, 5, 8, 12, 17, ... (+1, +2, +3, +4, +5)

(c) 1,   4,   9,   16,   25,   36,   ...
(1×1) (2×2) (3×3) (4×4) (5×5) (6×6)

(d) 2nd term: $2 \times 2 + 1 = 5$
3rd term: $5 \times 2 + 1 = 11$
4th term: $11 \times 2 + 1 = 23$
5th term: $23 \times 2 + 1 = 47$
6th term: $47 \times 2 + 1 = 95$
2, 5, 11, 23, 47, 95, ...

978-1-62399-072-5
Singapore Math Challenge

Example 2: Look at each pattern carefully and find the missing number.

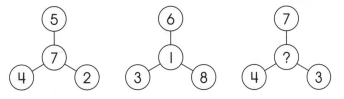

Solution:

$$4 + 5 = 9 = 7 + 2$$
$$3 + 6 = 9 = 1 + 8$$
$$7 + 4 = 11 = ? + 3$$
$$? = 11 - 3$$
$$= 8$$

Example 3: Look at each number pattern and find the unknown numbers.

(a)

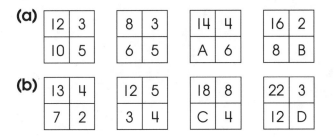

(b)

Solution:

(a) $12 + 3 = 15 = 10 + 5$
$8 + 3 = 11 = 6 + 5$
$14 + 4 = 18 = A + 6$ $16 + 2 = 18 = 8 + B$
$A = 18 - 6 = 12$ $B = 18 - 8 = 10$

(b) $7 + 4 = 11 = 13 - 2$
$3 + 5 = 8 = 12 - 4$
$18 - 4 = 14 = C + 8$ $12 + 3 = 15 = 22 - D$
$C = 14 - 8 = 6$ $D = 22 - 15 = 7$

Example 4: Look at each number pattern and find the unknown numbers.

(a)

2	2	8
3	2	10
5	3	A

(b)

6	4	4
8	3	10
10	3	B

Solution:

(a) $2 + 2 = 4$ $4 \times 2 = 8$

$3 + 2 = 5$ $5 \times 2 = 10$

$5 + 3 = 8$ $8 \times 2 = A$ $A = 16$

(b) $6 - 4 = 2$ $2 \times 2 = 4$

$8 - 3 = 5$ $5 \times 2 = 10$

$10 - 3 = 7$ $7 \times 2 = B$ $B = 14$

Example 5: Fill in the blanks with the correct answers.

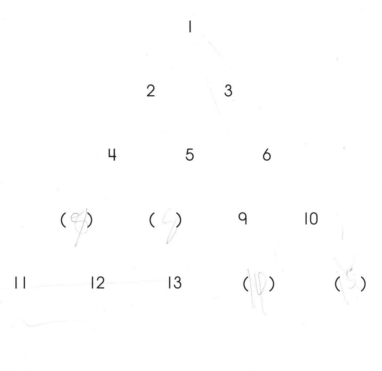

1

2   3

4   5   6

(7)   (8)   9   10

11   12   13   (14)   (15)

Solution:

    (7)   (8)   9   10

11   12   13   (14)   (15)

I. Complete each number pattern.

   (a) 4, 8, 12, 16, 20, (   ), (   ), ...

   (b) 1, 2, 4, (   ), 16, (   ), 64, ...

   (c) 1, 1, 2, 3, 5, (   ), (   ), ...

   (d) 2, 3, 5, 8, 13, (   ), (   ), ...

   (e) 3, 6, 9, (   ), 15, (   ), (   ), ...

   (f) 1, 4, 5, (   ), 14, 23, (   ), ...

   (g) 2, 3, 4, 6, (   ), (   ), ...

   (h) 3, 2, 5, 4, (   ), (   ), ...

   (i) 4, 5, 8, 13, (   ), (   ), ...

   (j) 2, 4, 8, 14, (   ), (   ), ...

978-1-62399-072-5
Singapore Math Challenge

2. Look at each pattern carefully and find the missing numbers.

(a)

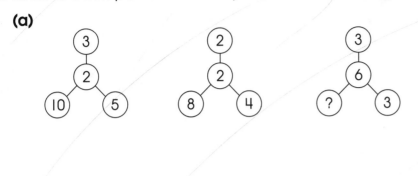

(b)

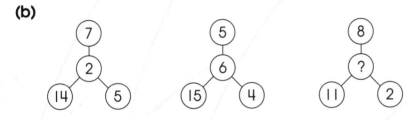

(c)

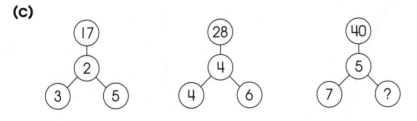

3. Which of the following number patterns shown below is not the same as the others?

(a) 2, 4, 6, 10, 16, ...

(b) 1, 2, 4, 8, 16, ...

(c) 1, 3, 4, 7, 11, 18, ...

4. Look at each number pattern and find the unknown numbers.

(a)

3	7
2	6

8	4
6	2

11	9
10	A

12	5
B	8

(b)

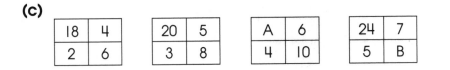

15	3
8	5

17	4
11	7

19	5
A	9

21	4
15	B

(c)

18	4
2	6

20	5
3	8

A	6
4	10

24	7
5	B

978-1-62399-072-5
Singapore Math Challenge

5. Fill in the blanks with the correct answers.

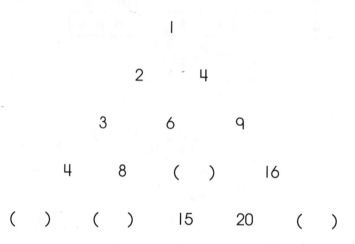

1

2   4

3   6   9

4   8   (   )   16

(   )   (   )   15   20   (   )

978-1-62399-072-5
Singapore Math Challenge

6. Fill in the blanks with the correct answers.

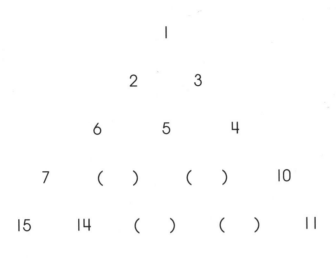

```
                    1

              2        3

          6       5       4

      7     (  )     (  )     10

   15    14     (  )     (  )     11
```

978-1-62399-072-5
Singapore Math Challenge

7. Look at each number pattern and find the missing numbers.

(a)

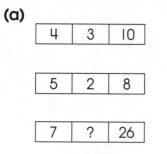

| 4 | 3 | 10 |

| 5 | 2 | 8 |

| 7 | ? | 26 |

(b)

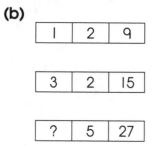

| 1 | 2 | 9 |

| 3 | 2 | 15 |

| ? | 5 | 27 |

978-1-62399-072-5
Singapore Math Challenge

8. Fill in each blank with the correct answer.

1	7	19		61	

		18		30	

9. Look at each number pattern and find the missing numbers.

(a)

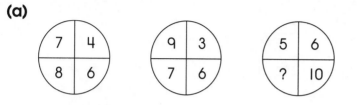

(b)

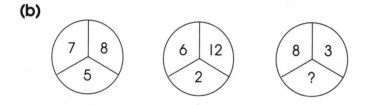

(c)

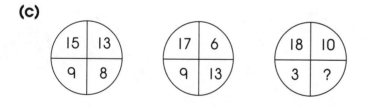

10. Look at each number pattern and find the unknown numbers.

(a)

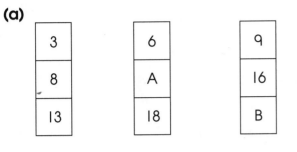

(b)

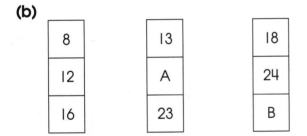

11. Find the unknown numbers.

(a)

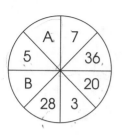

(b)

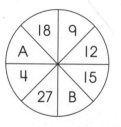

(c)

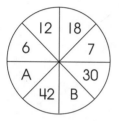

(d)

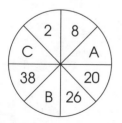

12. Look at each number pattern and find the unknown numbers.

(a)

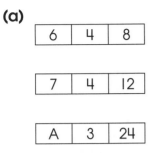

| 6 | 4 | 8 |

| 7 | 4 | 12 |

| A | 3 | 24 |

(b)

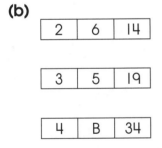

| 2 | 6 | 14 |

| 3 | 5 | 19 |

| 4 | B | 34 |

978-1-62399-072-5
Singapore Math Challenge

Counting

It is important to keep track of what we have already counted so we do not

- **(a)**   miss any numbers,
- **(b)**   repeat any numbers.

Example 1: How many squares are there in the figure below?

Solution:

Method 1

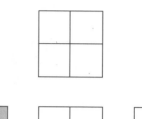

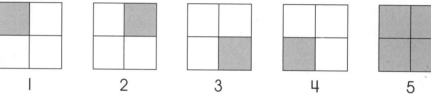

Method 2

Number of squares formed by 1 □ = 4
Number of squares formed by 4 □ s = 1
Total number of squares = 4 + 1 = 5
There are 5 squares in the figure.

978-1-62399-072-5
Singapore Math Challenge

Example 2: How many triangles are there in the figure below?

Solution:

Method 1

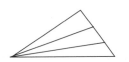

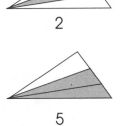
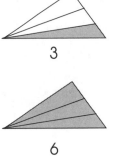
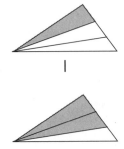

1   2   3

4   5   6

Method 2

Number of triangles formed by 1 △ = 3
Number of triangles formed by 2 △ s = 2
Number of triangles formed by 3 △ s = 1
Total number of triangles = 3 + 2 + 1 = 6
There are 6 triangles in the figure.

Example 3: How many cubes are there in the figure below?

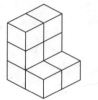

Solution:

Method 1: Count by Layers

3rd layer = 2   2nd layer = 2   1st layer = 4

2 + 2 + 4 = 8

Method 2: Count by Stacks

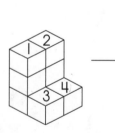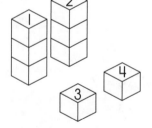

stack 1 = 3   stack 2 = 3
stack 3 = 1   stack 4 = 1
3 + 3 + 1 + 1 = 8
There are 8 cubes in the figure.

Example 4: How many lines of different lengths are there?

(a)

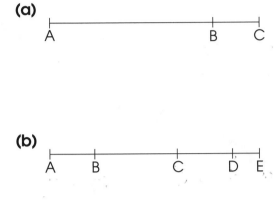

(b)

Solution:

(a)   Lines AB, BC and AC

There are 3 lines of different lengths.

(b)   Lines formed by:

1 line	2 lines	3 lines	4 lines
AB	AC	AD	AE
BC	BD	BE	
CD	CE		
DE			

4 + 3 + 2 + 1 = 10

There are 10 lines of different lengths.

I. How many squares are there in the figures below?

(a)

G

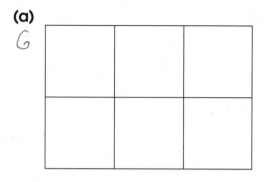

10 **(b)**

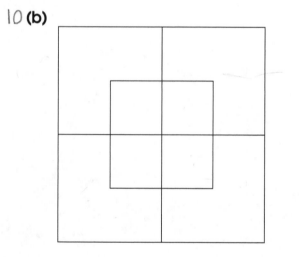

2. How many triangles are there in the figures below?

(a) 5

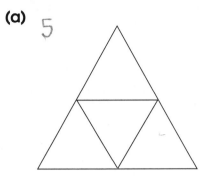

(b) 5

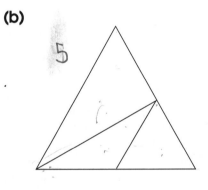

Name ______________________ Date ____________

3. How many rectangles are there in the figure below?

10

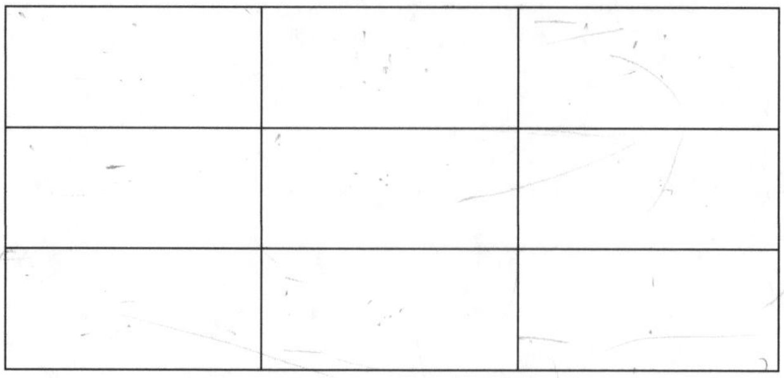

978-1-62399-072-5
Singapore Math Challenge

4. How many triangles are there in the figures below?

(a)

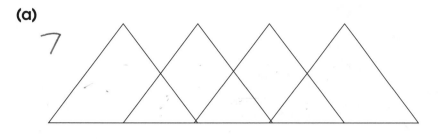

7

(b)

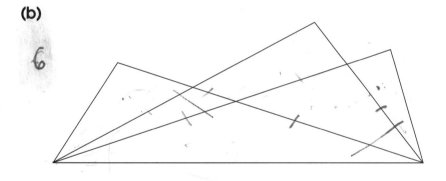

6

5. How many squares are there in the figure?
   How many triangles are there?

7 triangles

6 squares

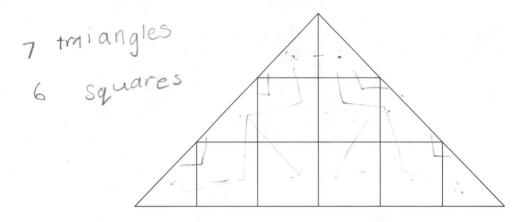

6. The figures shown below are formed by rectangles.
Count the number of rectangles in each figure.

(a)

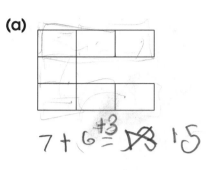

$7 + 6 = 15$

(b)

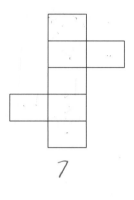

7

(c)

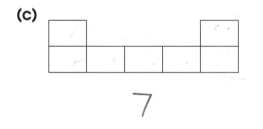

7

(d)

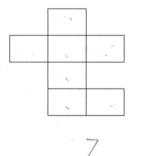

7

978-1-62399-072-5
Singapore Math Challenge

7. How many cubes are there in each of the following objects?

(a)

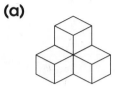

(b)

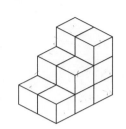

(c)

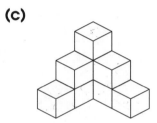

(d)

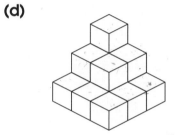

(e)

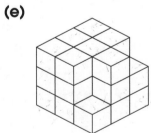

(f)

8. How many lines of different lengths are there in each of the following?

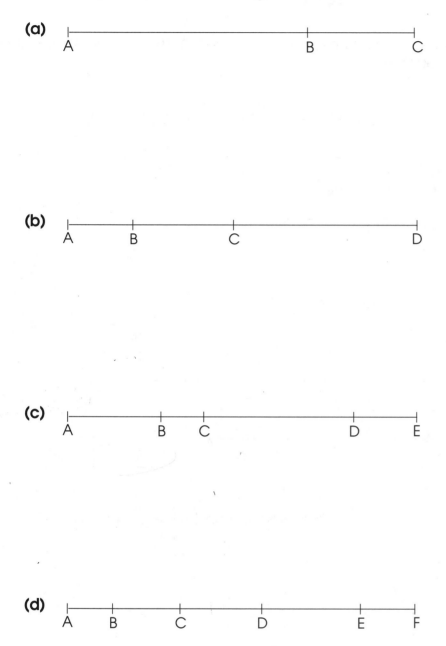

(a)

A   B   C

(b)

A   B   C   D

(c)

A   B   C   D   E

(d)

A   B   C   D   E   F

Logic

Logic problems deal mainly with reasoning skill rather than numbers. Tables are quite often used to sort out our thoughts.

Example 1: Alice, Benson, Charles and Natalie are lining up at their favorite restaurant.

Benson is second in line.
Charles is right in front of Alice.

What is the line number of each person?

Solution:

We can make a simple table to help us.

	1st	2nd	3rd	4th
Alice				✓
Benson		✓		
Charles			✓	
Natalie	✓			

Reasoning: Alice and Charles come in "a pair."

Natalie is first, Benson is second, Charles is third and Alice is fourth in the line.

Example 2: The jaguar, the black panther and the tiger decided to have a race one day.

The tiger did not come in first.
The black panther was neither the first nor the last one to finish the race.

Which animal was the slowest in the race?

Solution:

We make a table to help us by making a "✓" or a "✗" in the correct column.

	Fastest	2nd fastest	Slowest
Jaguar	✓		
Black Panther		✓	✗
Tiger	✗		✓

Reasoning: Since the panther was neither the first nor the last one in the race, it had to be in second place.

The tiger was the slowest in the race.

978-1-62399-072-5
Singapore Math Challenge

Example 3: The chocolate cake was half-eaten when Mrs. Jones returned from work. Below were her children's replies when they were being questioned.

Vanessa: I did not take it!
Melissa: Neither did I.
Bobby: Vanessa took the cake!

If two of her children lied, who ate the chocolate cake?

Solution:

We can use the Truth-Lie table to help us find out who ate the chocolate cake.

If Vanessa ate it,

	Lie	Truth
Vanessa	✓	
Melissa		✓
Bobby		✓

I child lied.

If Melissa ate it,

	Lie	Truth
Vanessa		✓
Melissa	✓	
Bobby	✓	

2 children lied.

If Bobby ate it,

	Lie	Truth
Vanessa		✓
Melissa		✓
Bobby	✓	

I child lied.

Melissa ate the chocolate cake.

1. During a baseball practice, Harry, Bill and Anthony each put on a cap of a different color.

Anthony is not wearing a yellow cap.
Bill's cap is neither yellow nor white.

Can you find out the color of the cap that each is putting on?
(Put a "✓" or a "×" in the appropriate box.)

	White	Yellow	Red
Harry			
Bill			
Anthony			

2. Wilfred, Kim and Shirley each have a favorite fruit.

Wilfred: I don't like oranges.
Kim: I don't eat apples or oranges.

Can you find out each person's favorite fruit?
(Put a "✓" or a "×" in the appropriate box.)

	Orange	Apple	Peach
Wilfred			
Kim			
Shirley			

978-1-62399-072-5
Singapore Math Challenge

3. Jolene, Jay and Jaclyn are different ages.

Jay is not the youngest.
Jaclyn is older than Jay.

Can you rank the children in order of age?
(Put a "✓" or a "×" in the appropriate box.)

	Youngest	2nd youngest	Oldest
Jolene			
Jay			
Jaclyn			

4. Rosemary, Melissa and Wendy each keep a pet dog.

The golden retriever does not belong to Wendy.
Neither the poodle nor the golden retriever belongs to Melissa.

Which pet dog does each girl keep?

	Golden retriever	Poodle	Dalmatian
Rosemary			
Melissa			
Wendy			

5. A basket, a steel bowl and a plastic bowl are used to contain different kinds of fruit.

The oranges are not placed in the plastic bowl.
The apples are not placed in the steel bowl.
The peaches are placed in neither the plastic bowl nor the basket.

Can you help to match the fruit to the correct containers?

	Oranges	Apples	Peaches
Basket			
Steel bowl			
Plastic bowl			

6. The children at a party were each given a balloon. The balloons could be either red, green or orange.

The red balloon did not belong to Jolene.
Betty did not manage to get the green one.
David did not receive the orange nor the red balloon.

Which colored balloon did each child get?

	Red	Green	Orange
Jolene			
Betty			
David			

7. Four rabbits took part in a 50-m race.

Flappy: **I beat Flower in the race.**
Pluffy: **I was slower than Flower.**
Clover: **Flappy was no match for me.**

Find out how the four rabbits did in the race.

8. Edward, Peter and Leon work in different professions. One is a dentist. The other two are either a teacher or a soldier.

Edward is older than the teacher.
Leon is not the same age as the teacher.
The soldier and Edward are good friends.

Can you figure out the profession of each man?

	Dentist	Teacher	Soldier
Edward			
Peter			
Leon			

978-1-62399-072-5
Singapore Math Challenge

9. A football flew toward Uncle Tommy's house and shattered his glass window. Three suspects were narrowed down.

Andrew: **Tommy threw that football, I promise.**
Billy: **I did not do it.**
Tommy: **Can someone tell me what is going on here?**

Two of the children lied. Who was the culprit?

If Andrew did it,

	Lie	Truth
Andrew		
Billy		
Tommy		

If Billy did it,

	Lie	Truth
Andrew		
Billy		
Tommy		

If Tommy did it,

	Lie	Truth
Andrew		
Billy		
Tommy		

978-1-62399-072-5
Singapore Math Challenge

10. 4 turtles took part in a 100-m race. Below were their replies when their friends checked up on how each of them was doing.

Fanfo: I was in neither the second place nor the last one to complete the race.
Momo: I was the best!
Round neck: I was beaten by none.
Long tail: I was faster than Momo.

One of the turtles did not tell the truth.
Reveal the results to their friends.

11. A paper airplane flew right onto the back of Mrs. Robinson's head as she was writing on the whiteboard. Three students were called to the principal's office for questioning.

Jimmy: I did not fly the airplane!
Randy: Jimmy did.
Peter: I don't know what is going on here!

Two of them lied to the principal.
Who flew the paper airplane?

If Jimmy did it,

	Lie	Truth
Jimmy		
Randy		
Peter		

If Randy did it,

	Lie	Truth
Jimmy		
Randy		
Peter		

If Peter did it,

	Lie	Truth
Jimmy		
Randy		
Peter		

978-1-62399-072-5
Singapore Math Challenge

12. There are 5 gift boxes of different sizes.

The red box is bigger than the white box.
The yellow box is bigger than the white box.
The black box is smaller than the red box.
The blue box is bigger than the yellow box but smaller than the black one.

Which box is the biggest?
Which box is the smallest?

978-1-62399-072-5
Singapore Math Challenge

Make a List, Make a Table

Example 1: In how many ways can an ant return home to point B from point A? Imagine it can only move → or ↑.

Solution:

We make a list of all the possible routes to return home.

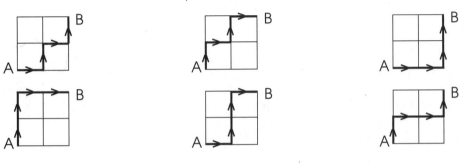

An ant can return home to point B from point A in 6 ways.

Example 2: How many multiples of 3 are between 8 and 32?

Solution:

We make a list of all the multiples of 3 between 8 and 32.

$3 \times 3 = 9$	$3 \times 4 = 12$	$3 \times 5 = 15$
$3 \times 6 = 18$	$3 \times 7 = 21$	$3 \times 8 = 24$
$3 \times 9 = 27$	$3 \times 10 = 30$	

8 multiples of 3 are between 8 and 32.

Example 3: The product of two numbers is 36.
The sum of the two numbers is 15.
Find the two numbers.

Solution:

We make a table to list all the possible numbers systematically.

1st number	1	2	3	4	6
2nd number	36	18	12	9	6

$3 + 12 = 15$

$3 \times 12 = 36$

The two numbers are 3 and 12.

978-1-62399-072-5
Singapore Math Challenge

Example 4: In how many ways can you form a 3-digit number using 1, 2 and 3 once each time?

Solution:

123 231 312

132 213 321

There are 6 ways to form a 3-digit number using 1, 2 and 3 once each time.

© Singapore Asia Publishers Pte Ltd   978-1-62399-072-5

Singapore Math Challenge

1. Arrange the objects in 5 more ways.

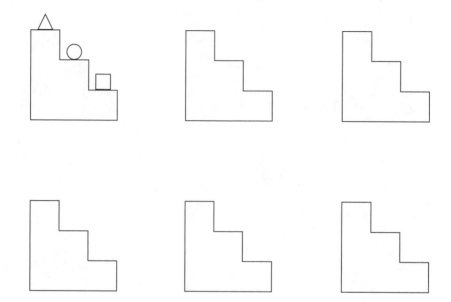

2. How many multiples of 4 are between 4 and 39?

3. A spider is positioned at point A.
   In how many ways can the spider return to point B?
   Use movements of →, ↑ and ↗ only.

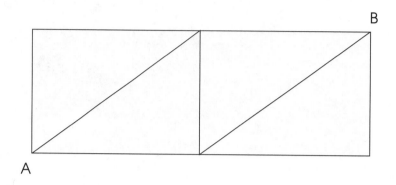

4. The product of two numbers is 48.
The sum of the two numbers is 16.
Find the two numbers.

5. Jonathan, together with his parents, is taking a family picture. Complete the table below to find out the possible sitting arrangements. The first one has been done for you.

1	Mom	Jonathan	Dad
2			
3			
4			
5			
6			

978-1-62399-072-5
Singapore Math Challenge

6. How many ways can you form the word "MAYOR" from the network shown below?

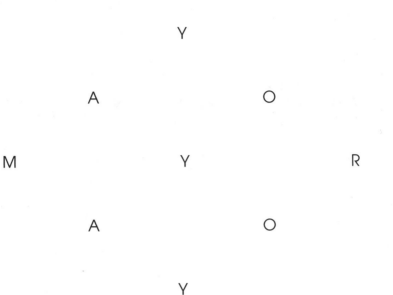

978-1-62399-072-5
Singapore Math Challenge

7. Hooray! Aunt Regina is going to treat Geoff to two movies on the same day. Below are the movies shown in the cinema.

1. Pets Next Door
2. Tommy and Jeffrey
3. The Wonder Cat
4. Mission Accomplished

It is a tough choice for Geoff. Can you find out the number of choices Geoff has?

8. How many triangles can you draw using any 3 dots shown below as the vertices (corners)?

9. The good news for an army of ants at point A is that food is available at point B. The bad news is that an anteater is waiting at point C.
How many ways can the ants reach point B safely without passing point C?
They can move either → or ↓ .

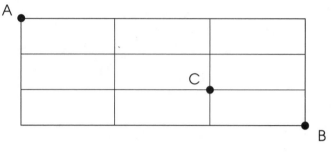

10. Wilfred has a twenty-cent stamp, a fifty-cent stamp and a one-dollar stamp. How many different postage amounts can he make with these stamps?

II. How many ways can you form the word "WATER" in the network shown below?

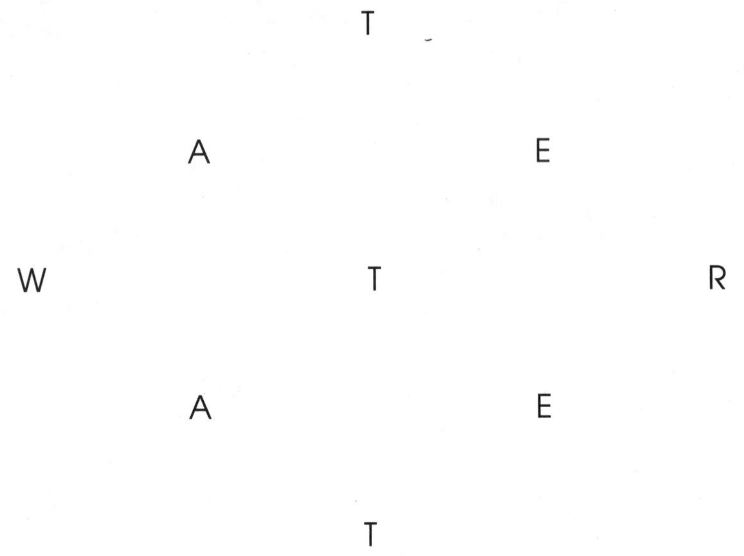

978-1-62399-072-5
Singapore Math Challenge

12. Leonard has seven 1-dollar bills, three 2-dollar bills and one 5-dollar bill. How many possible ways can Leonard make up a total value of $7? Find out by completing the table below.

No. of $1 bills	No. of $2 bills	No. of $5 bills	Total value
7	0	0	$7
5	1	0	$7
0	1	1	$7
1	3		$7
2	3	1	$7
			$7

978-1-62399-072-5
Singapore Math Challenge

13. Patrick did well on his report card. His dad decided to give him a treat. He had to choose one item each from the starter, main course and beverage menus.

Starter	Main Course	Beverage
1. Salad	A. Mexican Chicken	I. Soft drink
2. Clam Chowder	B. Italian Beef	II. Tea
	C. Braised Cod	III. Fruit juice

How many different combinations can he have?

14. There are 5 red balls, 5 white balls and 3 green balls in a bag. Nelson is blindfolded before he draws 3 balls from the bag.
List out all the possible results for the colors of balls he will draw out from the bag.

Using Models

Example 1: Amanda and Nancy have $60 altogether. Amanda has $10 more than Nancy. How much money does each of them have?

Solution:

$60 – $10 = $50

$50 ÷ $2 = $25

$25 + $10 = $35

Amanda has $35 and Nancy has $25.

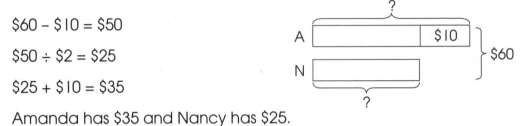

Example 2: The sum of two numbers is 100. The difference of the two numbers is 20. Find the two numbers.

Solution:

100 – 20 = 80

80 ÷ 2 = 40

40 + 20 = 60

The two numbers are 60 and 40.

Example 3: Natalie has 15 playing cards.
The number of playing cards Anne has is 3 times that of Natalie.
How many playing cards does Anne have?

Solution:

$15 + 15 + 15 = 45$

Anne has 45 cards.

N | 15 |

A | 15 | 15 | 15 |

?

Example 4: David and John have 100 marbles altogether.
The number of marbles David has is 4 times that of John.
How many marbles does each of them have?

Solution:

$100 \div 5 = 20$

$20 \times 4 = 80$

David has 80 marbles and John has 20 marbles.

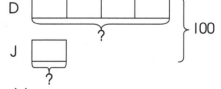

978-1-62399-072-5
Singapore Math Challenge

Example 5: Mr. Nelson has 24 chickens, geese and ducks altogether on his farm.
There are 4 more ducks than chickens.
There are 2 more geese than chickens.
Find the number of each farm animal Mr. Nelson has.

Solution:

$24 - 4 - 2 = 18$

$18 \div 3 = 6$ chickens

$6 + 2 = 8$ geese

$6 + 4 = 10$ ducks

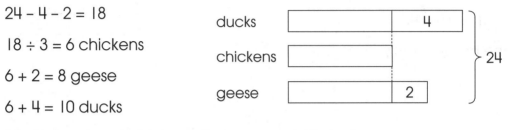

Mr. Nelson has 6 chickens, 8 geese and 10 ducks.

Example 6: Sheena has 26 birthday cards. Anne has 14 birthday cards.
How many birthday cards must Sheena give to Anne so that both will have the same number of birthday cards?

Solution:

$26 - 14 = 12$

$12 \div 2 = 6$

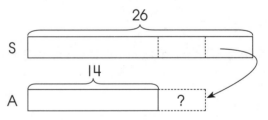

Sheena must give 6 birthday cards to Anne so that both will have the same number of birthday cards.

978-1-62399-072-5
Singapore Math Challenge

1. Split 110 beads into two bags so that one bag contains 10 more beads than the other one. How many beads are there in each bag?

2. The sum of two numbers is 200. The difference of the two numbers is 20. Find the two numbers.

3. Melvin and Edward have $80 altogether. Edward has $10 more than Melvin. How much money does each of them have?

4. Alison has $20. Anna has 4 times as much money as Alison. How much does Anna have?

5. Sherry and Louisa have 60 marbles altogether.
The number of marbles Sherry has is 3 times that of Louisa.
How many marbles does each of them have?

6. Two farmers have 140 chickens altogether.
The number of chickens Farmer A has is 6 times that of Farmer B.
How many chickens does each farmer have?

7. There are 57 pears, apples and peaches altogether in a big basket.
There are 3 fewer peaches than pears.
There are 6 more apples than peaches.
How many apples, pears and peaches are there?

8. Wilfred, Peter and Bobbie have $60 altogether.
Peter has $5 more than Wilfred.
Wilfred has $4 less than Bobbie.
How much does each of them have?

9. Bill has 30 storybooks. If he gives 4 storybooks to Jack, both of them will have the same number of storybooks.
How many storybooks does Jack have at first?

10. Two fish tanks contain 40 fish altogether.
The owner transfers 3 fish from the first fish tank to the other fish tank.
The two fish tanks now have the same number of fish.
How many fish are there in each fish tank at first?

978-1-62399-072-5
Singapore Math Challenge

11. Theater 1 has an audience of 120.
Theater 2 has an audience of 98.
How many spectators must move from theater 1 to theater 2 so that both theaters have the same number of audience members?

978-1-62399-072-5
Singapore Math Challenge

12. School buses A, B and C carry 42, 34 and 14 students respectively. How should the teacher reshuffle so that each school bus holds the same number of students?

13. There are 12, 19 and 11 parrots in cages A, B and C respectively. How should Alan arrange in order to have the same number of parrots in each cage?

14. Baskets A, B and C contain 25, 33 and 23 oranges respectively. How can you rearrange so that each basket contains the same number of oranges?

15. There are 40 eggs in two baskets altogether. If 5 eggs are transferred from the first to the second basket, the first basket will have 2 more eggs than the second one. How many eggs are in the second basket at first?

978-1-62399-072-5
Singapore Math Challenge

16. Some sparrows were perching on two branches of a tree. There were 5 more sparrows on the first branch at first. Then, 4 sparrows flew from the first branch to the second one. Which branch of the tree would have more sparrows? How many more sparrows were there?

In Search of a Series

The sum of a number sequence is called a series.
In this chapter, we shall learn about

- **(a)** how to find the series when all the numbers in a sequence are given;
- **(b)** how to find all the numbers in a sequence when its sum is given.

Example 1: Find the sum of the following number sequences.

- **(a)** $1 + 2 + 3 + 4 + 5$
- **(b)** $2 + 4 + 6 + 8 + 10$
- **(c)** $3 + 5 + 7 + 9 + 11$
- **(d)** $2 + 5 + 8 + 11 + 14$

Solution:

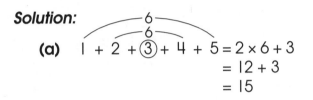

- **(a)**

$$1 + 2 + ③ + 4 + 5 = 2 \times 6 + 3$$
$$= 12 + 3$$
$$= 15$$

- **(b)**

$$2 + 4 + 6 + 8 + 10 = 10 \times 3$$
$$= 30$$

- **(c)**

$$3 + ⑤ + 7 + 9 + 11 = 5 + 10 + 20$$
$$= 35$$

- **(d)**

$$2 + ⑤ + 8 + 11 + 14 = 5 + 10 + 25$$
$$= 10 + 30$$
$$= 40$$

978-1-62399-072-5
Singapore Math Challenge

Example 2: The sum of five consecutive (continuous) numbers is 45. What are the five numbers?

Solution:

$$45 \div 5 = 9$$

9	9	9	9	9
↓	↓	↓	↓	↓
− 2	− 1		+ 1	+ 2
7	8	9	10	11

The five numbers are 7, 8, 9, 10 and 11.

Example 3: The sum of four consecutive odd numbers is 40. Find the four numbers.

Solution:

$$40 \div 4 = 10$$

10	10	10	10
↓	↓	↓	↓
− 3	− 1	+ 1	+ 3
7	9	11	13

The four numbers are 7, 9, 11 and 13.

Example 4: The sum of eight consecutive even numbers is 88. List all eight even numbers.

Solution:

$$88 \div 8 = 11$$

11	11	11	11	11	11	11	11
↓	↓	↓	↓	↓	↓	↓	↓
− 7	− 5	− 3	− 1	+ 1	+ 3	+ 5	+ 7
4	6	8	10	12	14	16	18

The eight even numbers are 4, 6, 8, 10, 12, 14, 16 and 18.

1. Use an easy method to work out each of the following series.

(a) $1 + 3 + 5 + 7 + 9$

(b) $7 + 10 + 13 + 16 + 19$

(c) $3 + 6 + 9 + 12 + 15 + 18$

(d) $3 + 4 + 5 + ... + 11 + 12$

2. Use a simple method to work out each of the following series.

(a) $1 + 4 + 7 + 10 + 13 + 16$

(b) $2 + 3 + 4 + ... + 11 + 12$

(c) $10 + 20 + 30 + 40 + 50$

(d) $1 + 2 + 3 + ... + 19 + 20$

978-1-62399-072-5
Singapore Math Challenge

3. The sum of three consecutive whole numbers is 24. List all three numbers.

4. The sum of five consecutive whole numbers is 50. List all five numbers.

5. The sum of nine consecutive whole numbers is 54. List all nine numbers.

978-1-62399-072-5
Singapore Math Challenge

6. The sum of seven consecutive whole numbers is 63. List all seven numbers.

978-1-62399-072-5
Singapore Math Challenge

7. Find the sum of the following series.

(a) 20 + 30 + 40 + ... + 70 + 80

(b) 3 + 5 + 7 + ... + 17 + 19 + 21

(c) 17 + 16 + 15 + ... + 4 + 3

(d) 11 + 12 + 13 + ... + 29 + 30

8. The sum of three consecutive odd numbers is 27. List all three odd numbers.

9. The sum of five consecutive odd numbers is 45. List all five odd numbers.

222

10. The sum of seven consecutive odd numbers is 63. List all seven odd numbers.

978-1-62399-072-5
Singapore Math Challenge

11. There are 10 seats in the first row, 12 seats in the second row, 14 seats in the third row ....
How many seats are there in the 10th row?

12. Phyllis read 4 pages of a storybook on the first day. She read 7 pages on the second day, 10 pages on the third day ....
If it took her 10 days to finish reading the storybook, how many pages were there in the storybook?

13.

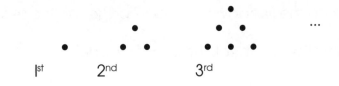

1st   2nd   3rd

(a) Draw the 4th and 5th patterns.

(b) How many dots are there altogether from the 1st to the 6th pattern?

14.

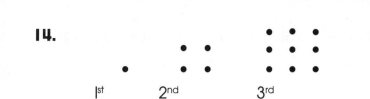

1st   2nd   3rd

(a) Draw the 4th and 5th patterns.

(b) How many dots are there altogether from the 1st to the 7th pattern?

978-1-62399-072-5
Singapore Math Challenge

15. The sum of seven consecutive even numbers is 56. Find all seven even numbers.

16. The sum of eight consecutive odd numbers is 64. Find all eight numbers.

17. The sum of four consecutive odd numbers is 40. Find all four numbers.

18. The sum of five consecutive even numbers is 40. Find all five numbers.

What Comes Next?

1. What comes next in each of the following patterns?
Draw and shade the 4ᵗʰ item in each of the following.

(a)

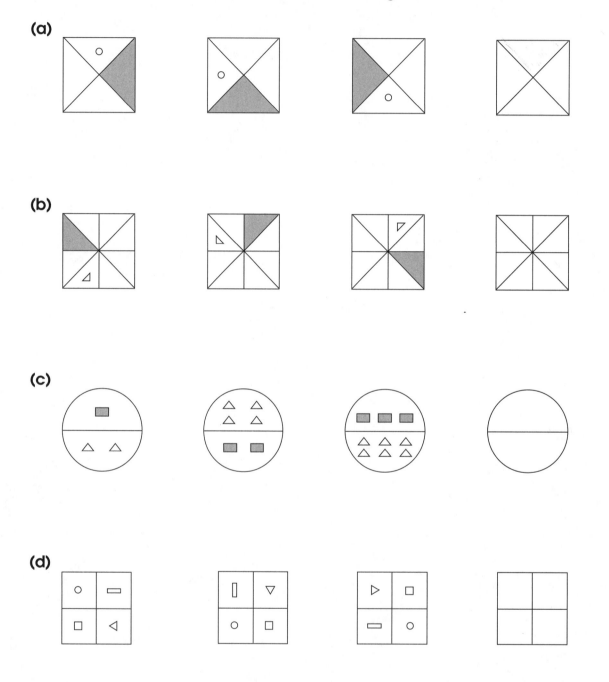

(b)

(c)

(d)

2. Complete the last pattern.

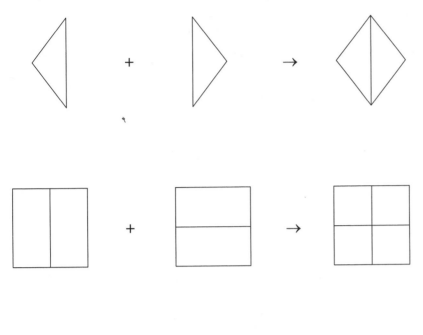

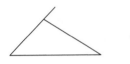

3. How would the 4th drawing look?

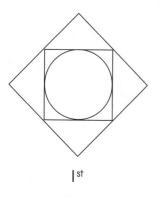

1st

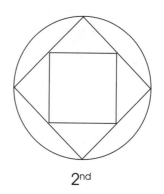

2nd

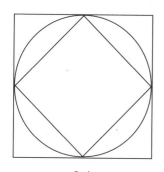

3rd

4th

978-1-62399-072-5
Singapore Math Challenge

4. Complete the pattern by drawing the correct symbols.

✳	○		Δ	✳		φ	Δ		
Δ	❖		φ	○		□	✳		
φ	□		□	❖		❖	○		

978-1-62399-072-5
Singapore Math Challenge

5. Complete the pattern below by drawing the correct symbols.

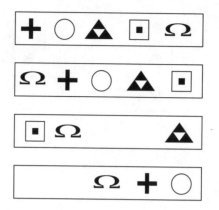

6. How would the next capsule look?

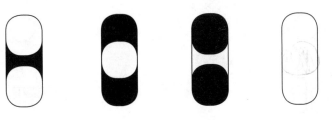

7. Complete the pattern below by drawing and shading the correct shape.

8. Complete the pattern below by drawing the missing figure.

9. Draw the 4ᵗʰ item in the pattern.

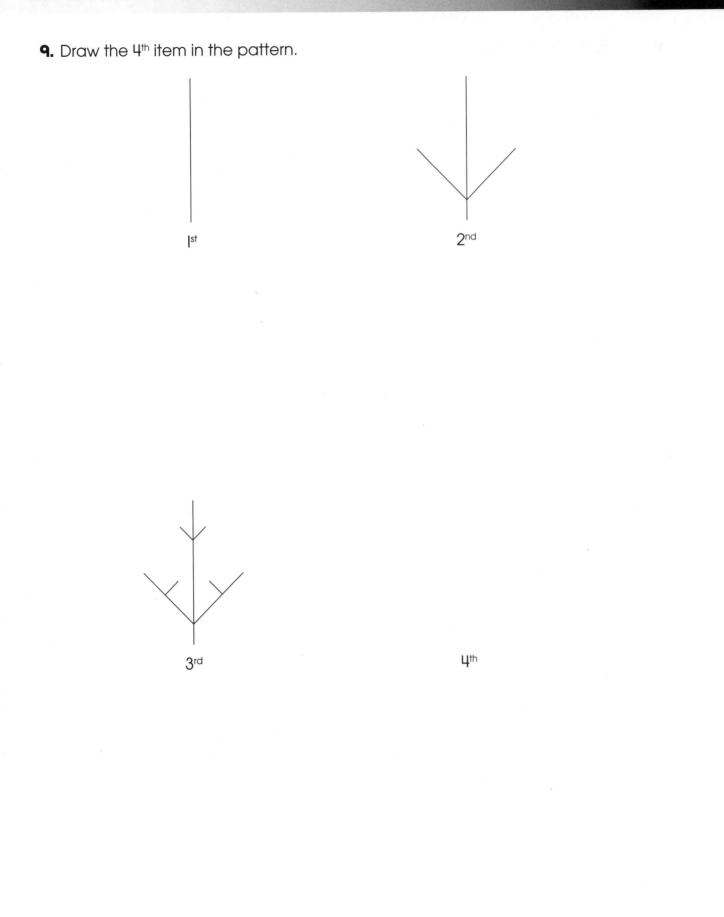

1st

2nd

3rd

4th

10. Shade the 2ⁿᵈ drawing in the pattern.

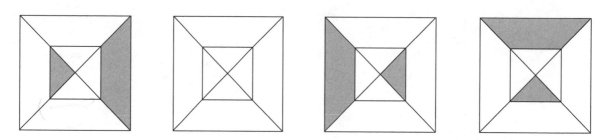

11. Which of the following figures is not the same as the rest?

A

B

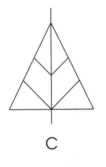

C

D

978-1-62399-072-5
Singapore Math Challenge

12. Draw the 4th figure in the pattern.

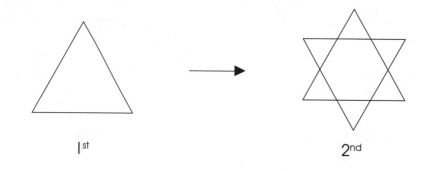

1st   2nd

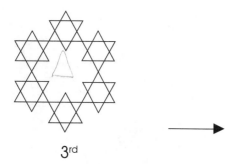

3rd   4th

13. Draw the 5ᵗʰ and 6ᵗʰ figures.

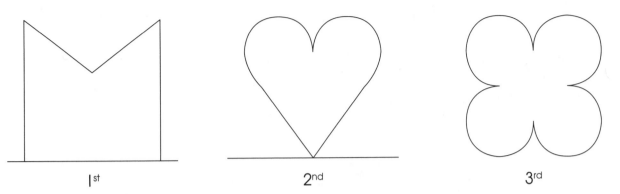

| 1st | 2nd | 3rd |

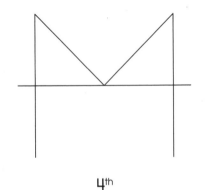

4ᵗʰ   5ᵗʰ   6ᵗʰ

978-1-62399-072-5
Singapore Math Challenge

14. What comes next? Draw the correct figure below.

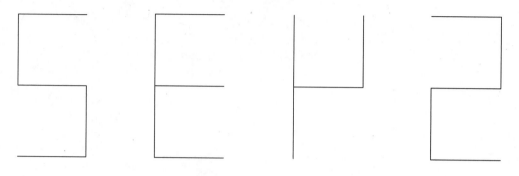

Math IQ

1. 35 marbles are to be put into 5 boxes.
The number of marbles in each box must be different and it must be an odd number.
How many marbles are there in each box?

978-1-62399-072-5
Singapore Math Challenge

2. Calvin has $50.
Given the price list of six different items, how many items can he buy at the most?
Assume that he can buy only one of each item.

Item	A	B	C	D	E	F
Price	$25	$10	$5	$8	$12	$20

3. How many " Is" can be found in numbers 1-50?

4. At a riverbank, 42 adventurers saw a rubber raft. The rubber raft can only ferry 6 people across the river at one time.
How many trips must be made in order to ferry all adventurers across the river?

5. There are 9 gold coins.
One of them, which is slightly lighter, is a fake.
How can you sort out the fake coin using a balance?

6. Mr. Clooney mixed up all the keys to 6 padlocks.
The keys looked the same.
How many attempts must be made at the most to find the right key to each padlock?

7. How many slices of pizza can you get at the most from 3 cuts of the pizza cutter?

8. The sum of the two facing page numbers of a storybook that Jaclyn is reading is 35. What are the two facing page numbers that Jaclyn is reading?

9. The product of the two facing page numbers of a comic that Bryan is reading is 132. What are the two facing page numbers that Bryan is reading?

10. Amanda broke the glass clock that her dad had just bought. The glass clock broke into 3 pieces. The sum of the 4 numbers on each shattered piece is 26. How was the glass clock broken?

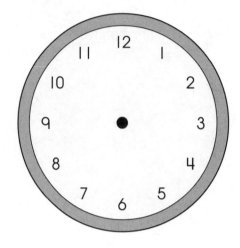

11. Divide the figure into two identical parts using a straight line. Color each part with a different color.

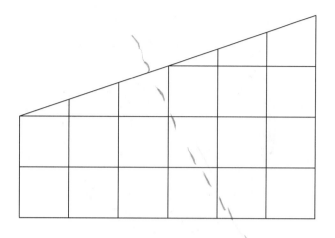

12. Divide the clock shown below into 6 regions so that the sum of the numbers in each region is the same.

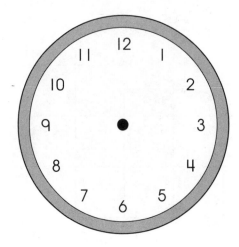

13. Divide the following shape into 4 identical parts.
Color each part with a different color.

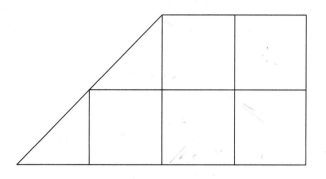

14. Which of the following figures can be formed using L-shaped tiles like the one shown below?

(a)

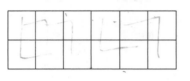

(b)

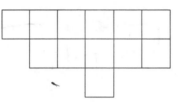

(c)

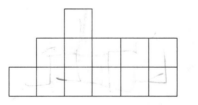

(d)

15. How can you arrange 12 pots of flowers alongside a square garden so that there are 4 pots of flowers on each side?

16. Fill in each box with a number so that the numbers will add up to 18 horizontally, vertically and diagonally.

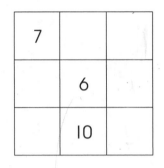

7		
	6	
	10	

17. Fill in each box with a number so that the numbers will add up to 24 horizontally, vertically and diagonally.

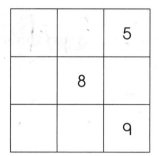

Geometry

(A) Cut and Paste

Example 1: In (a) and (b), cut along the dotted line to make the parts into a square.

(a)

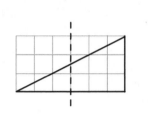

(b)

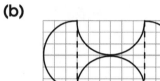

Solution:

(a)

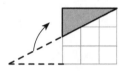

(b)

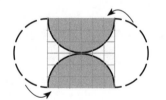

Example 2: Use at least 3 ways to cut the square into 2 equal parts.

Solution:

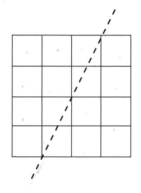
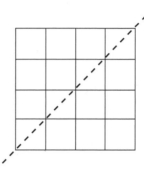
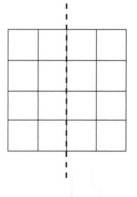

978-1-62399-072-5
Singapore Math Challenge

(B) Overlap

Example 1: Draw the correct figures when A is stacked with B.

(a)

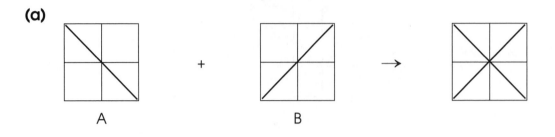

A   +   B   →

(b)

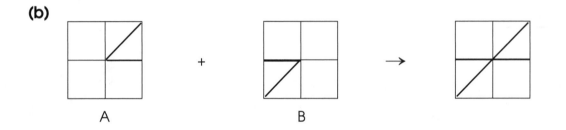

A   +   B   →

Example 2: Shade the correct boxes when A overlaps B.

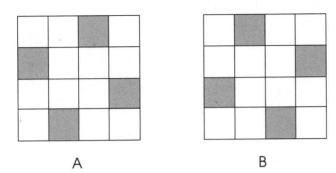

A   B

Solution:

1. The L-shaped figures below are made of 4 identical squares.
   Use 3 ways to divide each figure into 4 equal parts.

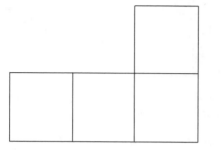
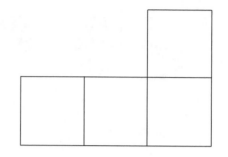

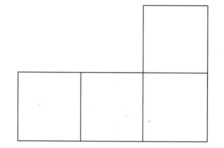

978-1-62399-072-5
Singapore Math Challenge

2. Use at least 4 ways to divide each big square into 4 equal parts.

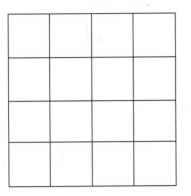
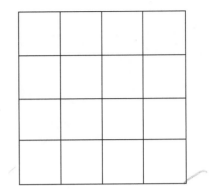

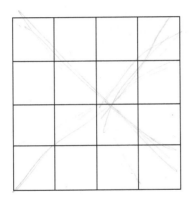
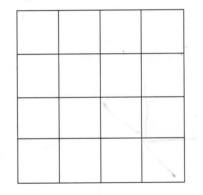

3. Divide the figure below into four identical shapes.

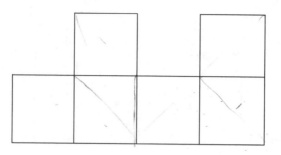

4. How would you cut each figure once and paste the two parts together to form a square?

(a)

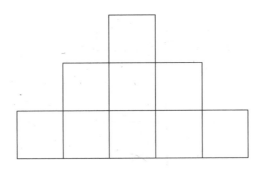

(b)

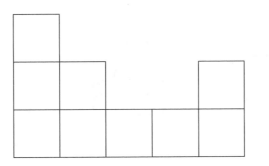

5. Use at least 2 ways to cut the figures below into 4 equal parts.

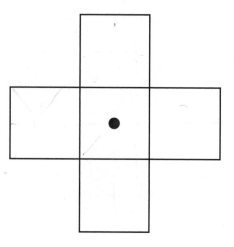

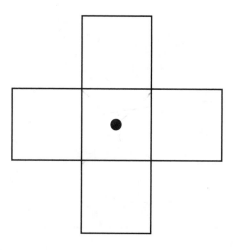

6. (a) Trace the drawing below on another piece of paper.

   (b) Cut along the dotted line.

   (c) Form 3 different shapes by pasting two pieces of paper together.

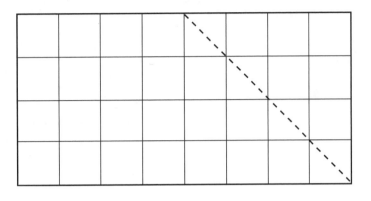

978-1-62399-072-5
Singapore Math Challenge

7. Divide the following triangles into

(a) 3 equal parts.

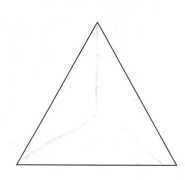

(b) 4 equal parts.

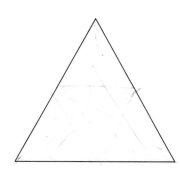

(c) 6 equal parts.

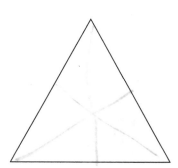

8. Draw the correct figure when A is stacked with B.

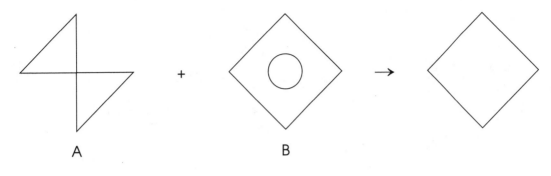

978-1-62399-072-5
Singapore Math Challenge

9. Draw the correct figure when A, B and C are stacked together.

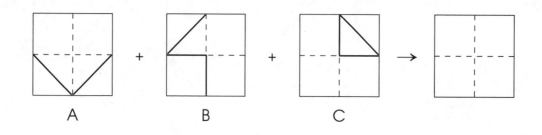

10. Draw the correct figure in the box below.

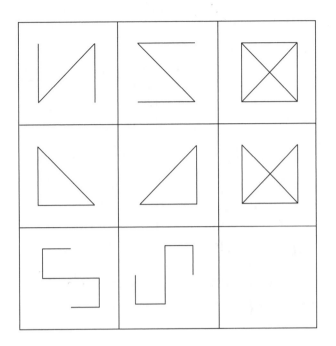

11. Shade the correct boxes.

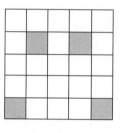

+

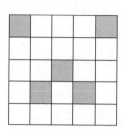

↓

12. Shade the correct boxes.

(a)

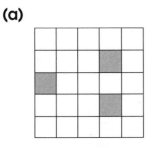

+

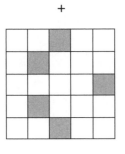

↓

(b)

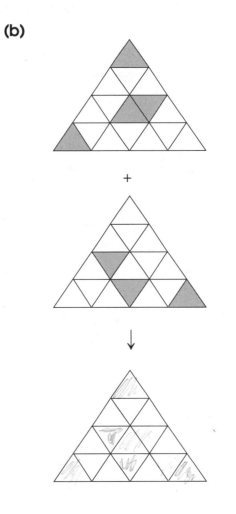

Odd and Even Numbers

1, 3, 5, 7, 9 ... are odd numbers.

2, 4, 6, 8, 10 ... are even numbers.

Remember that

   even number + even number = even number

   even number – even number = even number

   odd number + odd number = even number

   odd number – odd number = even number

   even number + odd number = odd number

   even number – odd number = odd number

Example 1: Are the results of the following addition and subtraction problems odd or even?

(a) 3 + 8

(b) 4 + 6

(c) 6 – 2

(d) 9 – 5

(e) 12 – 5

(f) 10 + 5

(g) 5 + 9

(h) 6 + 9

(i) 8 – 4

(j) 7 + 8

Solution:

(a) odd + even = odd

(b) even + even = even

(c) even – even = even

(d) odd – odd = even

(e) even – odd = odd

(f) even + odd = odd

(g) odd + odd = even

(h) even + odd = odd

(i) even – even= even

(j) odd + even = odd

Example 2: 12 apples are to be placed in 2 baskets. How many ways are there to place the apples so that each basket contains an odd number of apples?

Solution:

$$12 = 1 + 11$$
$$12 = 3 + 9$$
$$12 = 5 + 7$$

There are 3 ways to place the apples so that each basket contains an odd number of apples.

Example 3: Is the result of the series $1 + 2 + 3 + 4 + 5$ an odd or even number?

Solution:

$$1 \quad + \quad 2 \quad + \quad 3 \quad + \quad 4 \quad + \quad 5$$
$$\uparrow \qquad \uparrow \qquad \uparrow \qquad \uparrow \qquad \uparrow$$
odd   even   odd   even   odd

odd + even = odd

We have 3 odd numbers.

odd + odd + odd = odd

The result of the series is an odd number.

Example 4: A string of beads are strung in this manner.
blue, green, blue, green, blue, green ...
What is the color of the 15th bead?
What is the color of the 28th bead?

Solution:

blue,	green,	blue,	green,	blue,	green	...
↑	↑	↑	↑	↑	↑	
odd	even	odd	even	odd	even	

The 15th bead is an odd number so it is a blue bead.

The 28th is an even number so it is a green bead.

Example 5: Is the result of the series
10 + 11 + 12 + 13 + 14 + 15 + 16 + 17 + 18
an odd or even number?

Solution:

There are 5 even numbers and 4 odd numbers.

Sum of 5 even numbers → even number

Sum of 4 odd numbers → even number

even + even = even

The result of the series is an even number.

I. Are the results of the following addition and subtraction problems odd or even?

(a) 4 + 7

(b) 8 + 5

(c) 11 − 7

(d) 3 + 9

(e) 10 + 2

(f) 12 − 4

(g) 5 + 9

(h) 15 − 7

(i) 6 + 12

(j) 18 + 11

(k) 17 − 11

(l) 19 − 7

2. 16 marbles are to be given to 2 children. How many ways are there to give the marbles away so that each child will receive an odd number of marbles?

978-1-62399-072-5
Singapore Math Challenge

3. 14 oranges are to be placed in 2 baskets.
How many ways are there to place the oranges so that each basket contains an even number of oranges?

4. In the number sequence,
1, 3, 6, 10, 15, 21, 28 ....
Is the 15th term an odd or even number?
How about the 23rd term?

5. In the number sequence,
1, 4, 9, 16, 25, 36 ....
Is the 10th term odd or even?
Is the 15th term odd or even?

6. Is the result of the series 1 + 2 + 3 + ... + 9 + 10 odd or even?

7. The sum of 3 consecutive (continuous) odd numbers is 21. Find the 3 numbers.

978-1-62399-072-5
Singapore Math Challenge

8. How many ways are there to give 12 apples to 3 children so that each child will get an even number of apples?

9. Is the sum of the first 5 odd numbers odd or even?

10. Is the sum of the first 5 even numbers odd or even?

978-1-62399-072-5
Singapore Math Challenge

11. In the number sequence,
1, 1, 2, 3, 5, 8, 13 .... 21 34 55 89 144 233
Is the 16th term odd or even?
Is the 27th term odd or even?

12. How many tiles do you need to cover the area shown in each figure?

(a)

 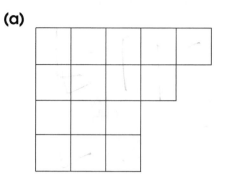

Tile:

(b)

Tile: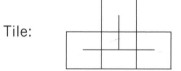

(c)

Tile: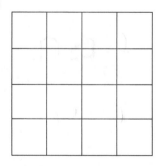

Ordinal Numbers

Example 1: What is the position of the penguin?
How about the kangaroo?

Solution:

The penguin is 5ᵗʰ in line.

The kangaroo is 2ⁿᵈ.

Example 2: Before playing a game, a group of children lined up in a room.
Anne was 5th from the left.
She was also 5th from the right.
How many children took part in this game?

Solution:

left ○ ○ ○ ○ ● ○ ○ ○ ○ right

                  ↑

               Anne

9 children took part in this game.

978-1-62399-072-5
Singapore Math Challenge

Name _____ Date _____

Example 3: Sharon was 6th in line. She was the 7th child if counted from the end of the line. How many children were in the line?

Solution:

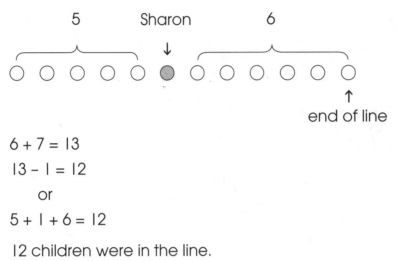

$6 + 7 = 13$

$13 - 1 = 12$

or

$5 + 1 + 6 = 12$

12 children were in the line.

296   978-1-62399-072-5
Singapore Math Challenge

Example 4: There were 5 people in front of Priscilla when she was in line for movie tickets. She was 9th from the end of the line. How many people were in line for movie tickets?

Solution:

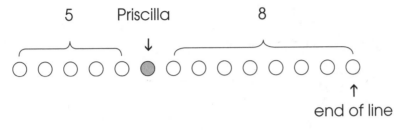

$$5 + 1 + 8 = 14$$

14 people were in line for movie tickets.

978-1-62399-072-5
Singapore Math Challenge

Example 5: Laura was 6th in a line.
Amanda was 6th from the end of the line.
There were 3 children between Laura and Amanda.
How many children were there in the line?

Solution:

Laura   Amanda
↓   ↓

○ ○ ○ ○ ○ ● ○ ○ ○ ● ○ ○ ○ ○ ○

6 + 3 + 6 = 15

There were 15 children in the line.

1. 8 cars were stuck in a traffic jam.
A red car was 5ᵗʰ in the traffic jam.
What was its position if we count from the back of the traffic jam?

2. In a line, there are 3 children in front of Melanie and 7 children behind her. How many children were in the line?

3. On a string, there are 7 white beads to the left of a black bead.
There are also 7 white beads to the right of the black bead.
How many beads are there altogether?

4. In the first row of a school choir, there are 3 members to the left of Tanya. There are 5 members to the right of Tanya.

How many choir members are in the first row?

5. Bruno was in line for his movie ticket. There were 15 people in the line. He was 9th in line.
In which position was he from the end of the line?

978-1-62399-072-5
Singapore Math Challenge

6. Mrs. George hangs 5 handkerchiefs side by side on a clothesline.
Each handkerchief uses 2 clothespins.
How many clothespins does she use altogether?

7. Jolene was 6th in a line. Amy was 8th in the same line but counted from the end of the line.
If there were 3 children between Jolene and Amy, how many children were in the line?

8. The first row of seats in a theater was fully occupied.
Robin was seated in the 6th place from the left in the first row.
Rosalind was seated in the 6th place from the right in the same row.
There were 4 children between Robin and Rosalind.
How many seats were in the first row?

9. There were 18 children in a line.
Vanessa was 3rd in the line.
Andrea was 6th from the end of the line.
How many children were between Vanessa and Andrea?

10. Two planks of wood of the same length are nailed together as shown below.
The total length then becomes 90 cm.
How long is each plank of wood?

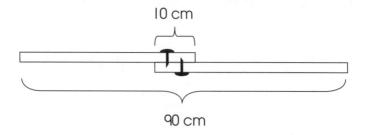

11. Two pieces of ribbon have the same length.
15 cm from each ribbon are used to tie a butterfly knot. The total length of the two ribbons then becomes 60 cm.
How long is each piece of ribbon?

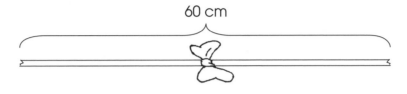

60 cm

12. 35 students took part in the freestyle swimming event.
23 students took part in the backstroke swimming event.
10 students took part in both events.
How many students took part in the events?

Solutions

Name

ach blank with the correct answer.

| I | 7 | 19 | | 61 | |

| | | 18 | | 30 | |

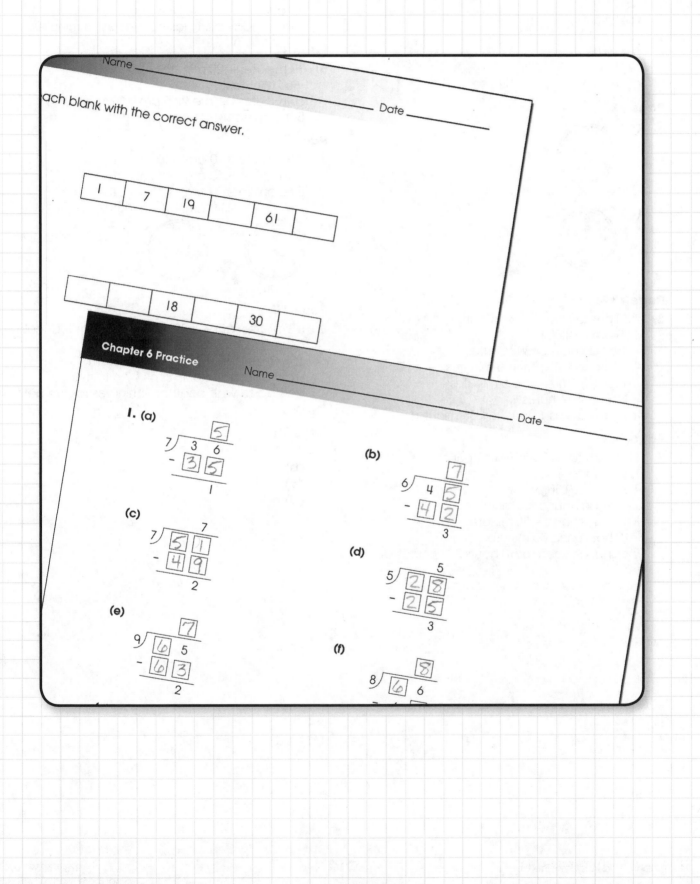

Chapter 6 Practice

Name _____

Date _____

I. (a)

$$7\overline{)36}$$ quotient 5, minus 35, remainder 1

(b)

$$6\overline{)45}$$ quotient 7, minus 42, remainder 3

(c)

$$7\overline{)51}$$ quotient 7, minus 49, remainder 2

(d)

$$5\overline{)28}$$ quotient 5, minus 25, remainder 3

(e)

$$9\overline{)65}$$ quotient 7, minus 63, remainder 2

(f)

$$8\overline{)66}$$ quotient 8, ... 6

Chapter 1 Practice

Page 11

1. **(a)** 7:15
   (b) 2:45
   (c) 4:55
   (d) 10:40
   (e) 5:50
   (f) 6:15

Page 12

2. **(a)**

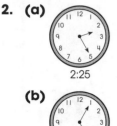

2:25

   (b)

5:05

Page 13

3. 2:30 pm to 3:30 pm → 1 hour
   3:30 pm to 4:00 pm
   → half an hour or 30 minutes
   4:00 pm to 4:05 pm → 5 minutes
   1 hour + 30 minutes + 5 minutes
   = 1 hour 35 minutes
   The movie was 1 hour and 35 minutes.

Page 14

4. 11:00 am to 12:00 pm → 1 hour
   12:00 pm to 9:00 pm → 9 hours
   9:00 pm to 9:30 pm
   → half an hour or 30 minutes
   1 hour + 9 hours + 30 minutes
   = 10 hours and 30 minutes
   The shop is open for 10 hours 30 minutes daily.

Page 15

5. 2:30 pm to 5:30 pm → 3 hours
   5:30 pm to 5:45 pm → 15 minutes
   3 hours + 15 minutes = 3 hours 15 minutes
   The birthday party lasted 3 hours 15 minutes.

Page 16

6. 10 minutes + 20 minutes + 20 minutes
   = 50 minutes
   50 minutes before 2:50 pm is 2 pm.
   Benson reached home at 2 pm.

Page 17

7. 7:20 am to 8:10 am → 50 minutes
   8:10 am to 8:50 am → 40 minutes
   8:50 am to 9:20 am → 30 minutes
   9:20 am to 9:40 am → 20 minutes

   9:20   9:40

Page 18

8. 8 minutes after 8:30 am is 8:38 am. Lincoln
   arrived at the bus stop at 8:38 am.
   15 minutes after 8:30 am is 8:45 am.
   From 8:38 am to 8:45 am → 7 minutes
   He had to wait another 7 minutes for the next
   bus.

Page 19

9. **(a)** 2:50
   (b) 8:15
   (c) 7:30
   (d) 5:45

Page 20

10. 40 minutes after 6:30 am → 7:10 am
40 minutes after 7:10 am → 7:50 am
The third train would leave at 7:50 am.

Page 21

11. *Method 1*

1st	2nd	3rd	4th	5th	6th	7th	8th	9th	10th	11th	trains
0	6	12	18	24	30	36	42	48	54	60	minutes

Method 2
$60 \div 6 = 10$
$10 + 1 = 11$
11 trains would have arrived at the subway station in 60 minutes.

Page 22

12. 1st bus → 5:00 am
2nd bus → 6:30 am
3rd bus → 8:00 am
4th bus → 9:30 am
The fourth bus leaves the station at 9:30 am.

Page 23

13. 1 + 2 + 3 + 4 + 5 + 6

$7 \times 3 = 21$
It would have chimed 21 times by 6 o'clock.

Page 24

14. starting time → 2 pm
ending time → 5:40 pm
Her birthday party was 3 hours and 40 minutes long.

978-1-62399-072-5
Singapore Math Challenge

Chapter 2 Practice

Page 28

1.

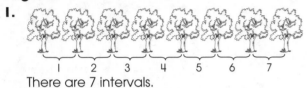

1   2   3   4   5   6   7

There are 7 intervals.

Page 29

2. There are 7 intervals along the road.
$7 \times 2 = 14$
There are 14 trees along that stretch of road.

Page 30

3. There are 3 intervals along the road.
$3 \times 3\,m = 9\,m$
The fourth tree is 9 m from the first one.

Page 31

4. There are 3 intervals from the first lamp post to the fourth one.
$3 \times 5\,m = 15\,m$
The fourth lamp post is 15 m from the first one.

Page 32

5. There are 4 intervals from the first knot to the fifth one.
$4 \times 20\,cm = 80\,cm$
The fifth knot is 80 cm from the first one.

Page 33

6.

1st   2nd   3rd   4th   5th   6th   7th

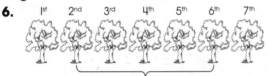

?

$4 \times 3\,m = 12\,m$
The sixth tree is 12 m from the second one.

Page 34

7. $8 \times 10\,cm = 80\,cm$
The ninth coin is 80 cm from the first one.

Page 35

8.

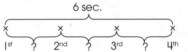

Peter needs to saw the plank of wood 3 times.
$3 \times 5\,min. = 15\,min.$
Peter will take 15 minutes to saw a plank of wood of the same length into four pieces.

Page 36

9.

6 sec.

1st   ?   2nd   ?   3rd   ?   4th

$6\,sec. \div 3 = 2\,sec.$
Each interval is 2 seconds.
$5 \times 2\,sec. = 10\,sec.$
The grandfather clock will take 10 seconds to chime 6 times at 6 o'clock.

Page 37

10. There are 4 staircases leading from the ground floor to the 5th floor.
$4 \times 10 = 40$
Alison has to climb 40 steps before she reaches home.

Page 38

11.

4×2 min. $= 8$ min.

The subway train takes 8 minutes to travel from the first to the fifth station.

3×1 min. $= 3$ min.

The subway train waits a total of 3 minutes at the station.

8 min. $+ 3$ min. $= 11$ min.

The subway train takes 11 minutes to travel from the first to the fifth station.

Page 39

12. 6m 6m 6m 6m 6m 6m

6×6 m $= 36$ m

(total length of all compartments)

5×1 m $= 5$ m

(total length of all connectors)

36 m $+ 5$ m $= 41$ m

The train is 41 m long.

Page 40

13.

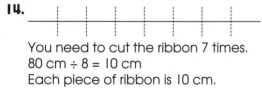

7 buses would have left the station in 60 minutes.

Page 41

14.

You need to cut the ribbon 7 times.

80 cm $\div 8 = 10$ cm

Each piece of ribbon is 10 cm.

Page 42

15. *Method 1*

$5 + 4 + 3 = 12$

Method 2

$3 \times 5 = 15$

$15 - 3 = 12$

Deduct 3 as the corners are counted twice.

Vanessa uses 12 coins to form the triangle.

Chapter 3 Practice

Page 47

1. (a) $2 + 8 + 3 + 7 = 10 + 10$
   $= 20$

   (b) $5 + 4 + 6 + 5 = 10 + 10$
   $= 20$

   (c) $9 + 2 + 8 + 1 = 10 + 10$
   $= 20$

   (d) $14 + 16 + 21 + 29 = 30 + 50$
   $= 80$

   (e) $13 + 28 + 22 + 17 = 30 + 50$
   $= 80$

   (f) $15 + 37 + 23 + 25 = 60 + 40$
   $= 100$

   (g) $26 + 14 + 33 + 37 = 40 + 70$
   $= 110$

   (h) $18 + 19 + 22 + 11 = 40 + 30$
   $= 70$

   (i) $28 + 32 + 15 + 25 = 60 + 40$
   $= 100$

   (j) $32 + 22 + 28 + 10 = 32 + 50 + 10$
   $= 92$

   (k) $42 + 16 + 15 + 18 = 60 + 16 + 4 + 11$
   $= 80 + 11$
   $= 91$

   (l) $18 + 13 + 22 + 28 = 18 + 2 + 11 + 50$
   $= 20 + 11 + 50$
   $= 81$

Page 48

2. (a) $9 + 8 + 10 = 10 - 1 + 10 - 2 + 10$
   $= 30 - 3$
   $= 27$

   (b) $7 + 8 + 9 = 10 - 3 + 10 - 2 + 10 - 1$
   $= 30 - 6$
   $= 24$

   (c) $7 + 8 + 9 + 11 = 7 + 3 + 5 + 20$
   $= 10 + 5 + 20$
   $= 35$

   (d) $10 + 19 + 17 = 10 + 20 - 1 + 20 - 3$
   $= 50 - 4$
   $= 46$

   (e) $18 + 19 + 20 = 20 - 2 + 20 - 1 + 20$
   $= 60 - 3$
   $= 57$

   (f) $9 + 19 + 39 = 10 - 1 + 20 - 1 + 40 - 1$
   $= 70 - 3$
   $= 67$

   (g) $18 + 28 + 38 = 20 - 2 + 30 - 2 + 40 - 2$
   $= 90 - 6$
   $= 84$

   (h) $16 + 17 + 18 + 19 = 10 + 3 + 2 + 1 + 17 + 18 + 19$
   $= 10 + 20 + 20 + 20$
   $= 70$

Page 49

3. **(a)** $18 + 19 + 13 = 18 + 19 + 2 + 1 + 10$
    $\underbrace{\quad}_{20}\underbrace{\quad}_{20}$
    $= 20 + 20 + 10$
    $= 50$

    (b) $17 + 18 + 15 = 17 + 18 + 3 + 2 + 10$
    $\underbrace{\quad}_{20}\underbrace{\quad}_{20}$
    $= 20 + 20 + 10$
    $= 50$

    (c) $21 + 22 + 23 + 24 = 20 + 1 + 20 + 2 + 20 + 3 + 20 + 4$
    $= 20 \times 4 + 1 + 2 + 3 + 4$
    $= 80 + 10 = 90$

    (d) $19 + 17 + 14 + 21 = 19 + 21 + 17 + 3 + 11$
    $= 40 + 20 + 11$
    $= 71$

    (e) $33 + 24 + 13 + 14$
    $= 30 + 3 + 20 + 4 + 10 + 3 + 14$
    $= 60 + 10 + 14$
    $= 84$

    (f) $28 + 23 + 9 + 22 = 50 + 22 + 1 + 9$
    $\underbrace{\quad}_{50}$
    $= 50 + 22 + 10$
    $= 82$

    (g) $29 + 23 + 28 + 16 = 29 + 1 + 20 + 2 + 28 + 16$
    $\underbrace{\quad}_{30}\qquad\underbrace{\quad}_{30}$
    $= 30 + 30 + 36$
    $= 96$

    (h) $27 + 4 + 29 + 35 = 27 + 3 + 1 + 29 + 35$
    $\underbrace{\quad}\quad\underbrace{\quad}$
    $= 30 + 30 + 35$
    $= 95$

Page 50

4. **(a)** $7 = 2 + 5$

    (b) $12 = 5 + 7$

    (c) $18 = 5 + 13$
    $18 = 7 + 11$

    (d) $36 = 13 + 23$
    $36 = 17 + 19$
    $36 = 29 + 7$

    (e) $42 = 19 + 23$
    $42 = 29 + 13$

    (f) $48 = 19 + 29$

Page 51

5. **(a)** $10 = 2 + 3 + 5$

    (b) $23 = 3 + 7 + 13 = 5 + 7 + 11$

    (c) $38 = 2 + 7 + 29 = 2 + 13 + 23$

    (d) $37 = 3 + 5 + 29 = 3 + 11 + 23$
    or $= 13 + 17 + 7$

    (e) $41 = 5 + 17 + 19 = 5 + 13 + 23$
    or $= 5 + 7 + 29 = 7 + 11 + 23$

    (f) $49 = 3 + 17 + 29 = 7 + 13 + 29$
    or $= 7 + 19 + 23 = 13 + 17 + 19$

Page 52

6. **(a)**
    $$\begin{array}{r} 2\ 3 \\ +\ 3\ 5 \\ \hline 5\ 8 \end{array}$$

    (b)
    $$\begin{array}{r} 2\ 7 \\ +\ 4\ 5 \\ \hline 7\ 2 \end{array}$$

    (c)
    $$\begin{array}{r} 1\ 8 \\ +\ 2\ 1 \\ \hline 3\ 9 \end{array}$$

    (d)
    $$\begin{array}{r} 3\ 1 \\ +\ 1\ 4 \\ \hline 4\ 5 \end{array}$$

    (e)
    $$\begin{array}{r} 2\ 4 \\ +\ 4\ 4 \\ \hline 6\ 8 \end{array}$$

    (f)
    $$\begin{array}{r} 2\ 7 \\ +\ 3\ 5 \\ \hline 6\ 2 \end{array}$$

    (g)
    $$\begin{array}{r} 5\ 7 \\ +\ 6\ 3 \\ \hline 1\ 2\ 0 \end{array}$$

    (h)
    $$\begin{array}{r} 8\ 2 \\ +\ 4\ 9 \\ \hline 1\ 3\ 1 \end{array}$$

Chapter 4 Practice

Page 56

1. 1 chicken $\rightarrow$ 2 squirrels
   1 squirrel $\rightarrow$ 12 eggs
   2 squirrels $\rightarrow$ 24 eggs
   1 chicken $\rightarrow$ 24 eggs

Page 57

2. 1 duck $\rightarrow$ 5 chicks
   2 ducks $\rightarrow$ 10 chicks
   2 ducks $\rightarrow$ 1 goose
   1 goose $\rightarrow$ 10 chicks

Page 58

3. $\bigcirc + \square + \bigcirc - \square = 14 + 6$
   $\bigcirc + \bigcirc + \square - \square = 20$
   $\bigcirc + \bigcirc = 20$
   $\bigcirc = 20 \div 2 = 10$
   $\square = 10 - 6 = 4$

Page 59

4. $\square + \triangle + \triangle - \square = 15 + 7$
   $\square - \square + \triangle + \triangle = 22$
   $\triangle + \triangle = 22$
   $\triangle = 22 \div 2 = 11$
   $\square = 11 - 7 = 4$

Page 60

5. $* - \square + * + \square = 22 + 30$
   $* + * + \square - \square = 52$
   $* + * = 52$
   $* = 52 \div 2 = 26$
   $\square = 26 - 22 = 4$

Page 61

6. $\clubsuit = 15 - 11 = 4$
   $* = 11 - 4 = 7$

Page 62

7. $\bigcirc + \bigcirc + \bigcirc + * = 22$
   $\bigcirc + \bigcirc + 12 = 22$
   $\bigcirc + \bigcirc = 22 - 12 = 10$
   $\bigcirc = 10 \div 2 = 5$
   $* = 12 - 5 = 7$

Page 63

8. $\clubsuit + \clubsuit + \clubsuit + * + * = 18$
   $\clubsuit + \clubsuit + 14 = 18$
   $\clubsuit + \clubsuit = 18 - 14 = 4$
   $\clubsuit = 4 \div 2 = 2$
   $* = (14 - 2) \div 2 = 6$

Page 64

9. $\square + \bigcirc + \bigcirc + \bigcirc + \bigcirc = 24$
   $14 + \bigcirc + \bigcirc = 24$
   $\bigcirc + \bigcirc = 24 - 14 = 10$
   $\bigcirc = 10 \div 2 = 5$
   $\square = 14 - 5 - 5 = 4$

Page 65

10. 1 pineapple $\rightarrow$ 3 oranges
    2 pineapples $\rightarrow$ 6 oranges
    2 oranges $\rightarrow$ 4 apples
    6 oranges $\rightarrow$ 12 apples
    2 pineapples $\rightarrow$ 12 apples
    1 pineapple $\rightarrow$ 6 apples

Page 66

11. 2 apples $\rightarrow$ 6 strawberries
    1 apple $\rightarrow$ 3 strawberries
    3 apples $\rightarrow$ 9 strawberries
    2 pears $\rightarrow$ 9 strawberries

Page 67

12. 1 watermelon $\rightarrow$ 16 apples
    2 apples $\rightarrow$ 3 apricots
    16 apples $\rightarrow$ 24 apricots
    1 watermelon $\rightarrow$ 24 apricots

978-1-62399-072-5
Singapore Math Challenge

Page 68

13. ✳ + ✳ + ❖ + ❖ + ❖ = 58

$$22$$
$$22$$

$$22 + 22 + ❖ = 58$$
$$44 + ❖ = 58$$
❖ = 58 − 44 = 14
✳ = 22 − 14 = 8

Page 69

14. ✳ + ✳ + ✳ + ○ + ○ = 65

$$25$$
$$25$$

✳ + 25 + 25 = 65
✳ + 50 = 65
✳ = 65 − 50 = 15
○ = 25 − 15 = 10

Page 70

15. ❖ + ❖ + □ + □ + ○ + ○
= 9 + 12 + 11 = 32
❖ + □ + ○ = 16
□ = 16 − 9 = 7
❖ = 16 − 12 = 4
○ = 16 − 11 = 5

Page 71

16. 9 + 9 = 18 = 6 + 6 + 6
9 + 6 + 6 + 6 = 33
❖ = 9
△ = 6

Page 72

17. △ = 17 − 11 = 6

Page 73

18. 8 × 4 = 32
8 + 8 + 8 = 24 = 32 − 8
○ = 4

Page 74

19. ✳ = 3
○ = 8
❖ = 9
□ = 5

Page 75

20. ✳ = 2
◇ = 6
○ = 5

978-1-62399-072-5
Singapore Math Challenge

Chapter 5 Practice

Page 79

1. My grandmother was 25 years older than my mother 5 years ago.

Page 80

2. 36 – 4 = 32
Chloe will be 32 years younger than her father in 8 years' time.

Page 81

3. 35 + 12 = 47
62 + 12 = 74
Her grandfather will be 74 years old. Her father will be 47 years old.

Page 82

4. 11 – 6 = 5
His brother is 5 years older than Tom.
Tom will be 5 years younger than his brother in 10 years' time.

Page 83

5. 22 ÷ 2 = 11
Valerie's sister is 11 years old.
85 – 22 – 11 = 52
Their father is 52 years old.

Page 84

6. Now: 56 + 31 + 7 = 94
One year later: 57 + 32 + 8 = 97
Two years later: 58 + 33 + 9 = 100
The sum of our ages will be 100 in 2 years' time.

Page 85

7. 7 × 4 = 28
His father is 28 years old.

Page 86

8. 7 × 5 = 35
His father was 35 years old when Teddy was 5 years old.
40 – 35 = 5
5 + 5 = 10
Teddy will be 10 years old when his father is 40 years old.

Page 87

9. Now: 42 + 36 + 7 = 85
One year later: 85 + 3 = 88
Two years later: 88 + 3 = 91
Three years later: 91 + 3 = 94
Four years later: 94 + 3 = 97
Five years later: 97 + 3 = 100
The sum of all their ages will be 100 in 5 years' time.

Page 88

10.

Phyllis's age	Father's age	Multiple
5	40	8 times
6	41	✗
7	42	6 times

7 – 5 = 2   or   42 – 40 = 2
Her father's age will be 6 times Phyllis's age in 2 years' time.

Page 89

11.

Anna's age	Mother's age	Multiple
5	33	✗
6	34	✗
7	35	5 times

7 – 5 = 2   or   35 – 33 = 2
Her mother's age will be 5 times her age in 2 years' time.

978-1-62399-072-5
Singapore Math Challenge

Page 90

12. $6 + 9 = 15$

Wendy will be 15 years old in 9 years' time.

$40 - 15 = 25$

Her sister will be 25 years old in 9 years' time.

$25 - 9 = 16$

Wendy's sister is 16 years old.

Page 91

13. $95 - 5 - 5 = 85$

The sum of their present ages is 85 years.

$85 = 45 + 40$

Mrs. Gibson is 40 years old and Mr. Gibson is 45 years old.

Page 92

14. $38 + 4 = 42$

Mr. Woody is 42 years old.

Now:	$42 + 38 + 8 = 88$
One year later:	$88 + 3 = 91$
Two years later:	$91 + 3 = 94$
Three years later:	$94 + 3 = 97$
Four years later:	$97 + 3 = 100$

The sum of all their ages will be 100 four years from now.

978-1-62399-072-5
Singapore Math Challenge

Chapter 6 practice

Page 99

1.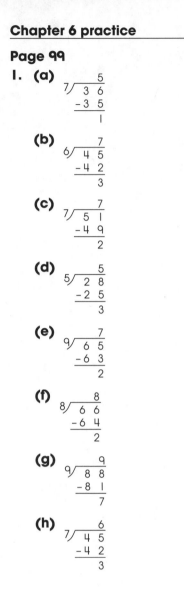
   (a)
   $$7\overline{)36}$$
   -35
   1

   (b)
   $$6\overline{)45}$$
   -42
   3

   (c)
   $$7\overline{)51}$$
   -49
   2

   (d)
   $$5\overline{)28}$$
   -25
   3

   (e)
   $$9\overline{)65}$$
   -63
   2

   (f)
   $$8\overline{)66}$$
   -64
   2

   (g)
   $$9\overline{)88}$$
   -81
   7

   (h)
   $$7\overline{)45}$$
   -42
   3

Page 100

2. **(a)** $26 \div 3 = 8\,R\,2$ or
   $26 \div 8 = 3\,R\,2$ or
   $26 \div 4 = 6\,R\,2$ or
   $26 \div 6 = 4\,R\,2$
   (b) $39 \div 4 = 9\,R\,3$ or
   $39 \div 6 = 6\,R\,3$ or
   $39 \div 9 = 4\,R\,3$
   (c) $47 \div 5 = 9\,R\,2$ or
   $47 \div 9 = 5\,R\,2$
   (d) $58 \div 6 = 9\,R\,4$ or
   $58 \div 9 = 6\,R\,4$
   (e) $68 \div 7 = 9\,R\,5$ or
   $68 \div 9 = 7\,R\,5$
   (f) $78 \div 8 = 9\,R\,6$ or
   $78 \div 9 = 8\,R\,6$

Page 101

3. **(a)** $31 \div 6 = 5\,R\,1$
   (b) $50 \div 7 = 7\,R\,1$
   (c) $57 \div 8 = 7\,R\,1$
   (d) $64 \div 9 = 7\,R\,1$

Page 102

4. **(a)** $17 \div 3 = 5\,R\,2$
   (b) $39 \div 5 = 7\,R\,4$
   (c) $27 \div 4 = 6\,R\,3$
   (d) $35 \div 6 = 5\,R\,5$
   (e) $47 \div 6 = 7\,R\,5$
   (f) $62 \div 7 = 8\,R\,6$

Page 103

5. **(a)** $29 \div 5 = 5\,R\,4$
   (b) $31 \div 4 = 7\,R\,3$
   (c) $41 \div 6 = 6\,R\,5$
   (d) $44 \div 5 = 8\,R\,4$
   (e) $39 \div 4 = 9\,R\,3$
   (f) $59 \div 6 = 9\,R\,5$

Page 104

6. $35 \div 6 = 5\,R\,5$
$28 \div 6 = 4\,R\,4$
$21 \div 6 = 3\,R\,3$
$14 \div 6 = 2\,R\,2$
$7 \div 6 = 1\,R\,1$

Page 105

7. ○ ● ◉
R1 R2 R0

$23 \div 3 = 7\,R\,2$
The color of the 23rd bead is gray.

$31 \div 3 = 10\,R\,1$
The color of the 31st bead is white.

Page 106

8. ○ ○ □ □ □
R1 R2 R3 R4 R0

$26 \div 5 = 5\,R\,1$
The shape of the 26th figure is ○.

$33 \div 5 = 6\,R\,3$
The shape of the 33rd figure is □.

Page 107

9. Charmaine   Shola   Amy
    R1   R2   R0

$34 \div 3 = 11\,R\,1$
Charmaine will get the last card.

Page 108

10. Jolene   Anna   Jim
   R1   R2, R3   R0

$1 + 2 + 1 = 4$
$54 \div 4 = 13\,R\,2$
Anna will get the last marble.

Page 109

11. 1   3   2   4
R1   R2   R3   R0

$27 \div 4 = 6\,R\,3$
The 27th number is 2.
$42 \div 4 = 10\,R\,2$
The 42nd number is 3.

Page 110

12. 3 red   2 orange   1 pink
R1, R2, R3   R4, R5   R0

$38 \div 6 = 6\,R\,2$
The color of the 38th lantern is red.
$58 \div 6 = 9\,R\,4$
The color of the 58th lantern is orange.

Page 111

13. *Method 1: Solve by Reasoning*
Sun. Mon. Tue. Wed. Thur. Fri. Sat.
R5   R6   R0   R1   R2   R3   R4
$23 \div 7 = 3\,R\,2$

Method 2: Draw a Table

Sun.	Mon.	Tue.	Wed.	Thur.	Fri.	Sat.
			1	2	3	4
5	6	7	8	9	10	11
12	13	14	15	16	17	18
19	20	21	22	23		

May 23rd was a Thursday that year.

978-1-62399-072-5
Singapore Math Challenge

Page 112

14. *Method 1: Solve by Reasoning*

March 20th to end of March: 12 days

April 1st to April 11th: 11 days

| Sun. | Mon. | Tue. | Wed. | Thur. | Fri. | Sat. |
| R1 | R2 | R3 | R4 | R5 | R6 | R0 |

$12 + 11 = 23$ $23 \div 7 = 3 \text{ R } 2$

Method 2: Draw a Table

Sun.	Mon.	Tue.	Wed.	Thur.	Fri.	Sat.
20	21	22	23	24	25	26
27	28	29	30	31	1	2
3	4	5	6	7	8	9
10	11					

April 11th was a Monday that year.

Page 113

15. We shall list out the multiples of 3 and 5.

3, 6, 9, 12, 15, 18, ...

5, 10, 15, 20, ...

Add 1 to each multiple of 3 and 5.

4, 7, 10, 13, ⑯, 19, ...

6, 11, ⑯, 21, ...

The common 2-digit number is 16.

$16 \div 5 = 3 \text{ R } 1$ $16 \div 3 = 5 \text{ R } 1$

The 2-digit number is 16.

Page 114

16. We shall list out the multiples of 4 and 5.

4, 8, 12, 16, 20, ...

5, 10, 15, 20, ...

Add 2 to each multiple of 4 and 5.

6, 10, 14, 18, ㉒, ...

7, 12, 17, ㉒, ...

The common 2-digit number is 22.

$22 \div 4 = 5 \text{ R } 2$ $22 \div 5 = 4 \text{ R } 2$

The 2-digit number is 22.

Chapter 7 Practice

Page 122

1. *Method 1: Solve by Drawing*

If we count all as motorcycles,

$8 \times 2 = 16$

$26 - 16 = 10$

Method 2: Make a Table

No. of cars	No. of wheels	No. of motorcycles	No. of wheels	Total no. of wheels
4	$4 \times 4 = 16$	4	$4 \times 2 = 8$	$16 + 8 = 24$
5	$5 \times 4 = 20$	3	$3 \times 2 = 6$	$20 + 6 = 26$

5 cars and 3 motorcycles are in the parking lot.

Page 123

2. *Method 1: Solve by Drawing*

If we count all as child movie tickets,

$5 \times \$5 = \$25$

$\$31 - \$25 = \$6$

Method 2: Make a Table

No. of adult movie tickets	Value	No. of child movie tickets	Value	Total value
3	$3 \times \$8 = \$24$	2	$2 \times \$5 = \$10$	$\$24 + \$10 = \$34$
2	$2 \times \$8 = \$16$	3	$3 \times \$5 = \$15$	$\$16 + \$15 = \$31$

He bought 2 adult movie tickets and 3 child movie tickets.

Page 124

3. *Method 1: Solve by Drawing*

If we count all as books on adventures,

$6 \times \$3 = \$18$

$\$26 - \$18 = \$8$

Method 2: Make a Table

No. of science fiction books	Value	No. of books on adventures	Value	Total value
3	$3 \times \$5 = \$15$	3	$3 \times \$3 = \$9$	$\$15 + \$9 = \$24$
4	$4 \times \$5 = \$20$	2	$2 \times \$3 = \$6$	$\$20 + \$6 = \$26$

She bought 4 science fiction books and 2 books on adventures.

Page 125

4. *Method 1: Solve by Drawing*

If we count all as bicycles,

$8 \times 2 = 16$

$22 - 16 = 6$

Method 2: Make a Table

No. of bicycles	No. of wheels	No. of tricycles	No. of wheels	Total no. of wheels
4	$4 \times 2 = 8$	4	$4 \times 3 = 12$	$8 + 12 = 20$
3	$3 \times 2 = 6$	5	$5 \times 3 = 15$	$6 + 15 = 21$
2	$2 \times 2 = 4$	6	$6 \times 3 = 18$	$4 + 18 = 22$

There are 6 tricycles and 2 bicycles.

Page 126

5. *Method 1: Solve by Drawing*

If we count all as chickens,

$12 \times 2 = 24$

$34 - 24 = 10$

Method 2: Make a Table

No. of chickens	No. of legs	No. of rabbits	No. of legs	Total no. of legs
6	$6 \times 2 = 12$	6	$6 \times 4 = 24$	$12 + 24 = 36$
7	$7 \times 2 = 14$	5	$5 \times 4 = 20$	$14 + 20 = 34$

The farmer has 5 rabbits and 7 chickens.

Page 127

6. *Method 1: Make a Table*

No. of chickens	No. of legs	No. of rabbits	No. of legs	Total no. of legs
8	$8 \times 2 = 16$	9	$9 \times 4 = 36$	$16 + 36 = 52$

Method 2: Solve by Assuming

Step 1: If all were chickens,

$17 \times 2 = 34$

$52 - 34 = 18$

there will be a shortage of 18 legs as some rabbits are counted as chickens.

Step 2: $4 - 2 = 2$

The difference in the number of legs between a chicken and a rabbit is 2.

Step 3: $18 \div 2 = 9$ rabbits

$17 - 9 = 8$ chickens

She has 9 rabbits and 8 chickens.

Page 128

7. *Method 1: Make a Table*

No. of big boxes	No. of marbles	No. of small boxes	No. of marbles	Total no. of marbles
5	$5 \times 12 = 60$	5	$5 \times 6 = 30$	$60 + 30 = 90$
4	$4 \times 12 = 48$	6	$6 \times 6 = 36$	$48 + 36 = 84$

Method 2: Solve by Assuming

Step 1: If all were big boxes,

$12 \times 10 = 120$

$120 - 84 = 36$

there will be an excess of 36 marbles as some small boxes are counted as big.

Step 2: $12 - 6 = 6$

The difference in the number of marbles that a big and a small box can hold is 6.

Step 3: $36 \div 6 = 6$ small boxes

$10 - 6 = 4$ big boxes

There are 4 big boxes and 6 small boxes.

Page 129

8. *Method 1: Solve by Drawing*

We count all as dragonflies,

$6 \times 10 = 60$

$68 - 60 = 8$

Method 2: Solve by Assuming

Step 1: If all were spiders,

$8 \times 10 = 80$

$80 - 68 = 12$

there will be an excess of 12 legs as some spiders are counted as dragonflies.

Step 2: $8 - 6 = 2$

The difference in the number of legs between a spider and a dragonfly is 2.

Step 3: $12 \div 2 = 6$ dragonflies

$10 - 6 = 4$ spiders

There are 4 spiders and 6 dragonflies.

Page 130

9. *Method 1: Solve by Drawing*
   Assume all were one-dollar postcards,

   | $1 | $1 | $1 | $1 | $1 | $1 | $1 | $1 | $1 | $1 | $1 |

   $11 \times \$1 = \$11$

   | $2 | $2 | $2 | $2 | $2 | $1 | $1 | $1 | $1 | $1 | $1 |

   $\$16 - \$11 = \$5$

   Method 2: Solve by Assuming
   Step 1: If all were two-dollar postcards,
   $$11 \times \$2 = \$22$$
   $$\$22 - \$16 = \$6$$
   there will be an excess of $6 as some one-dollar postcards are counted as two-dollar postcards.

   Step 2: $\$2 - \$1 = \$1$
   The difference in the value of the two types of postcards is $1.

   Step 3: $\$6 \div \$1 = 6$ one-dollar postcards
   $11 - 6 = 5$ two-dollar postcards
   He bought 5 two-dollar postcards and 6 one-dollar postcards.

Page 131

10. *Method 1: Make a Table*

No. of trucks	No. of wheels	No. of cars	No. of wheels	Total no. of wheels
7	$7 \times 6 = 42$	7	$7 \times 4 = 28$	$42 + 28 = 70$
8	$8 \times 6 = 48$	6	$6 \times 4 = 24$	$48 + 24 = 72$

   Method 2: Solve by Assuming
   Step 1: If all were trucks,
   $$14 \times 6 = 84$$
   $$84 - 72 = 12$$
   there will be an excess of 12 wheels as some cars are counted as trucks.

   Step 2: $6 - 4 = 2$
   The difference in the number of wheels between a truck and a car is 2.

   Step 3: $12 \div 2 = 6$ cars
   $14 - 6 = 8$ trucks
   There are 8 trucks and 6 cars.

Chapter 8 Practice

Page 136

1. **(a)** 4, 8, 12, 16, 20, 24, 28, ...
   Each term increases by 4.

   (b) 1, 2, 4, 8, 16, 32, 64, ...
   Each term is the multiplication of 2 and its previous term.

   (c) 1, 1, 2, 3, 5, 8, 13, ...
   Each term is the addition of the previous 2 terms.

   (d) 2, 3, 5, 8, 13, 21, 34, ...
   Each term is the addition of the previous 2 terms.

   (e) 3, 6, 9, 12, 15, 18, 21, ...
   Each term is a multiple of 3.

   (f) 1, 4, 5, 9, 14, 23, 37, ...
   Each term is the addition of the previous 2 terms.

   (g) 2, 3, 4, 6, 9, 14, ...
   $2 + 3 - 1 = 4$
   $3 + 4 - 1 = 6$
   $4 + 6 - 1 = 9$
   $6 + 9 - 1 = 14$

   (h) 3, 2, 5, 4, 7, 6, ...
   There are 2 sequences, the odd numbers and the even numbers.

   (i) 4, 5, 8, 13, 20, 29, ...
   $+1, +3, +5, +7, +9$

   (j) 2, 4, 8, 14, 22, 32, ...
   $+2, +4, +6, +8, +10$

Page 137

2. **(a)** $10 - 2 = 8 = 3 + 5$
   $8 - 2 = 6 = 2 + 4$
   $? - 6 = 6 = 3 + 3$
   $? = 12$

   (b) $14 - 2 = 12 = 7 + 5$
   $15 - 6 = 9 = 5 + 4$
   $11 - ? = 10 = 8 + 2$
   $? = 1$

   (c) $17 - 2 = 15 = 3 \times 5$
   $28 - 4 = 24 = 4 \times 6$
   $40 - 5 = 35 = 7 \times ?$
   $? = 5$

Page 138

3. **(a)** 2, 4, 6, 10, 16, ...
   $2 + 4 = 6$
   $4 + 6 = 10$
   $6 + 10 = 16$
   Each term is the addition of the 2 previous terms.

   (c) 1, 3, 4, 7, 11, 18, ...
   $1 + 3 = 4$
   $3 + 4 = 7$
   $4 + 7 = 11$
   $7 + 11 = 18$
   Each term is the addition of the 2 previous terms.

   Ans: (b) is not the same as (a) and (c).

Page 139

4. **(a)** $3 + 6 = 9 = 2 + 7$
   $8 + 2 = 10 = 6 + 4$
   $11 + A = 19 = 10 + 9$
   $A = 8$
   $12 + 8 = 20 = B + 5$
   $B = 15$

   (b) $8 - 3 = 5$ $5 + 10 = 15$
   $11 - 4 = 7$ $7 + 10 = 17$
   $A - 5 = 9$ $9 + 10 = 19$
   $A = 14$
   $15 - 4 = 11$ $B + 10 = 21$
   $B = 11$

   (c) $2 + 4 = 6$ $6 + 12 = 18$
   $3 + 5 = 8$ $8 + 12 = 20$
   $4 + 6 = 10$ $10 + 12 = A$
   $A = 22$
   $5 + 7 = 12$ $B + 12 = 24$
   $B = 12$

978-1-62399-072-5
Singapore Math Challenge

Page 140

5.

```
              1
          2       4
       3      6      9
     4    8   (12)    16
  (5)  (10)   15   20   (25)
```

Page 141

6.

```
                1
            2       3
          6    5     4
        7   (8)  (9)   10
     15   14  (13)  (12)  11
```

Page 142

7. **(a)** $4 \times 3 - 2 = 10$ $5 \times 2 - 2 = 8$
　　　$7 \times ? - 2 = 26$
　　　$? = 4$

　　(b) $1 + 2 = 3$　　$3 \times 3 = 9$
　　　$3 + 2 = 5$　　$5 \times 3 = 15$
　　　$? + 5 = 9$　　$9 \times 3 = 27$
　　　$? = 4$

Page 143

8.

1	7	19	37	61	91

$\underset{+6}{\frown}\underset{+12}{\frown}\underset{+18}{\frown}\underset{+24}{\frown}\underset{+30}{\frown}$

Each term is added by multiples of 6.

6	12	18	24	30	36

Each term is a multiple of 6.

Page 144

9. **(a)** $7 + 4 + 8 + 6 = 25$
　　　$9 + 3 + 7 + 6 = 25$
　　　$? + 5 + 6 + 10 = 25$
　　　$? = 25 - 21 = 4$

　　(b) $7 + 8 + 5 = 20$
　　　$6 + 12 + 2 = 20$
　　　$8 + 3 + ? = 20$
　　　$? = 20 - 11 = 9$

　　(c) $15 + 8 + 9 + 13 = 45$
　　　$17 + 13 + 6 + 9 = 45$
　　　$18 + ? + 10 + 3 = 45$
　　　$? = 45 - 31 = 14$

Page 145

10. **(a)**

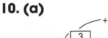
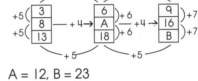

A = 12, B = 23

　　(b)

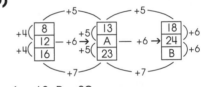

A = 18, B = 30

978-1-62399-072-5
Singapore Math Challenge

Page 146

11. (a) $5 \times 4 = 20$ $7 \times 4 = 28$
$3 \times 4 = A$ $B \times 4 = 36$
$A = 12$ $B = 36 \div 4 = 9$

(b) $6 + 24 = 30$ $18 + 24 = 42$
$12 + 24 = B$ $7 + 24 = A$
$B = 36$ $A = 31$

(c) $9 \times 3 = 27$ $4 \times 3 = 12$
$B \times 3 = 18$ $A \times 3 = 15$
$B = 6$ $A = 5$

(d) $A = 8 + 6 = 14$
$B = 26 + 6 = 32$
$C = 38 + 6 = 44$

Page 147

12. (a) $6 - 4 = 2$ $2 \times 4 = 8$
$7 - 4 = 3$ $3 \times 4 = 12$
$24 \div 3 = 8$ $A = 8 + 3 = 11$

(b) $2 \times 6 + 2 = 14$
$3 \times 5 + 4 = 19$
$4 \times B + 6 = 34$
$4 \times B = 34 - 6 = 28$
$B = 28 \div 4 = 7$

978-1-62399-072-5
Singapore Math Challenge

Chapter 9 Practice

Page 152

1. **(a)** Number of squares formed by 1☐ = 6
   Number of squares formed by 4☐s = 2
   Total number of squares = 8
   (b) Number of squares formed by 1☐ = 8
   Number of squares formed by 4☐s = 2
   Total number of squares = 10

Page 153

2. **(a)** Number of triangles formed by 1△ = 4
   Number of triangles formed by 4△s = 1
   Total number of triangles = 5
   (b) Number of triangles formed by 1△ = 3
   Number of triangles formed by 2△s = 1
   Number of triangles formed by 3△s = 1
   Total number of triangles = 5

Page 154

3. Number of rectangles formed by
   1☐ = 9
   2☐s : (a) 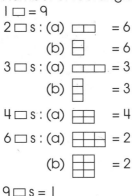 = 6
       (b) = 6
   3☐s : (a) = 3
       (b) = 3
   4☐s : (a) = 4
   6☐s : (a) = 2
       (b) = 2
   9☐s = 1
   Total number of rectangles = 36

Page 155

4. **(a)** Number of big triangles = 4
   Number of small triangles = 3
   Total number of triangles = 7
   (b) Number of triangles formed by
   1 △   = 5
   2 △s   = 4
   1 △ and 1 ▱   = 2
   3 △s   = 2
   3 △s and 1 ▱   = 1
   Total number of triangles = 14

Page 156

5. Number of squares formed by
   1 ☐ = 6
   4 ☐s = 1
   Total number of squares = 7
   Number of triangles formed by
   1 △   = 6
   2 △s (at the tip) = 1
   4 △s and 2 ☐s   = 1
   2 △s and 1 ☐   = 4
   3 △s and 3 ☐s   = 2
             all   = 1
   Total number of triangles = 15

Page 157

6. **(a)** Number of rectangles formed by
   1 ☐ = 7
   2 ☐s = 6
   3 ☐s = 3
   Total number of rectangles = 16
   (b) Number of rectangles formed by
   1 ☐ = 7
   2 ☐s = 6
   3 ☐s = 3
   4 ☐s = 2
   5 ☐s = 1
   Total number of rectangles = 19
   (c) Number of rectangles formed by
   1 ☐ = 7
   2 ☐s = 6
   3 ☐s = 3
   4 ☐s = 2
   5 ☐s = 1
   Total number of rectangles = 19
   (d) Number of rectangles formed by
   1 ☐ = 7
   2 ☐s = 6
   3 ☐s = 3
   4 ☐s = 1
   Total number of rectangles = 17

Page 158

7. **(a)** 1 + 3 = 4 cubes

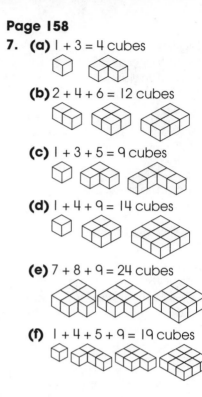

(b) 2 + 4 + 6 = 12 cubes

(c) 1 + 3 + 5 = 9 cubes

(d) 1 + 4 + 9 = 14 cubes

(e) 7 + 8 + 9 = 24 cubes

(f) 1 + 4 + 5 + 9 = 19 cubes

Page 159

8. **(a)** AB, BC, AC
There are 3 lines of different lengths.
(b) AB, BC, CD, AC, BD, AD
There are 6 lines of different lengths.
(c) AB, BC, CD, DE, AC, BD, CE,
AD, BE, AE
There are 10 lines of different lengths.
(d) AB, BC, CD, DE, EF,
AC, BD, CE, DF,
AD, BE, CF,
AE, BF,
AF
5 + 4 + 3 + 2 + 1 = 15
There are 15 lines of different lengths.

Chapter 10 Practice

Page 163

1.

	White	Yellow	Red
Harry		✓	
Bill	✗	✗	✓
Anthony	✓	✗	

Harry's cap is yellow, Bill's cap is red and Anthony's cap is white.

Page 164

2.

	Orange	Apple	Peach
Wilfred	✗	✓	
Kim	✗	✗	✓
Shirley	✓		

Wilfred's favorite fruit is apple, Kim's is peach and Shirley's is orange.

Page 165

3.

	Youngest	2nd youngest	Oldest
Jolene	✓		
Jay	✗	✓	
Jaclyn			✓

Jolene is the youngest, Jay is the second youngest and Jaclyn is the oldest.

Page 166

4.

	Golden retriever	Poodle	Dalmatian
Rosemary	✓		
Melissa	✗	✗	✓
Wendy	✗		✓

Rosemary keeps the Golden retriever, Melissa keeps the Dalmation and Wendy keeps the Poodle.

Page 167

5.

	Oranges	Apples	Peaches
Basket	✓		✗
Steel bowl	✗	✗	✓
Plastic bowl	✗	✓	✗

The container of the oranges is the basket.
The container of the apples is the plastic bowl.
The container of the peaches is the steel bowl.

Page 168

6.

	Red	Green	Orange
Jolene	✗		✓
Betty	✓	✗	
David	✗	✓	✗

Jolene got the orange balloon, Betty got the red balloon and David got the green balloon.

Page 169

7.

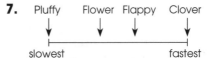

Clover is the fastest followed by Flappy, Flower and Pluffy.

Page 170

8.

	Dentist	Teacher	Soldier
Edward	✓	✗	✗
Peter		✓	
Leon		✗	✓

Edward is a dentist, Peter is a teacher and Leon is a soldier.

Page 171

9. If Andrew did it,

	Lie	Truth
Andrew	✓	
Billy		✓
Tommy		✓

If Billy did it,

	Lie	Truth
Andrew	✓	
Billy	✓	
Tommy		✓

If Tommy did it,

	Lie	Truth
Andrew		✓
Billy		✓
Tommy	✓	

Billy was the culprit.

Page 172

10. Momo could not have told the truth, otherwise Round neck and Long tail would be lying. So, Momo lied.

slowest ————————————— fastest

Momo Fanfo Long tail Round neck

Page 173

11. If Jimmy did it,

	Lie	Truth
Jimmy	✓	
Randy		✓
Peter		✓

If Randy did it,

	Lie	Truth
Jimmy		✓
Randy	✓	
Peter		✓

If Peter did it,

	Lie	Truth
Jimmy		✓
Randy	✓	
Peter	✓	

Peter flew the paper airplane.

Page 174

12. Start from the last clue.

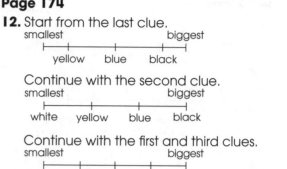

Continue with the second clue.

Continue with the first and third clues.

The red box is the biggest while the white box is the smallest.

Chapter 11 Practice

Page 178

1.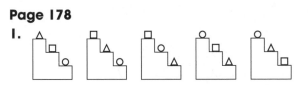

Page 179

2. Make a list of multiples of 4.
8, 12, 16, 20, 24, 28, 32, 36
8 multiples of 4 are between 4 and 39.

Page 180

3.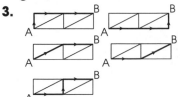

The spider can return to point B in 5 ways.

Page 181

4.

1st number	1	2	3	4	6
2nd number	48	24	16	12	8

The two numbers are 4 and 12.

Page 182

5.

1	Mom	Jonathan	Dad
2	Mom	Dad	Jonathan
3	Jonathan	Dad	Mom
4	Jonathan	Mom	Dad
5	Dad	Jonathan	Mom
6	Dad	Mom	Jonathan

Page 183

6.

The word "MAYOR" can be formed in 6 ways.

Page 184

7. His choices are:
1. Pets Next Door; Tommy and Jeffrey
2. Pets Next Door; The Wonder Cat
3. Pets Next Door; Mission Accomplished
4. Tommy and Jeffrey; The Wonder Cat
5. Tommy and Jeffrey; Mission Accomplished
6. The Wonder Cat; Mission Accomplished
Geoff has 6 choices.

Page 185

8.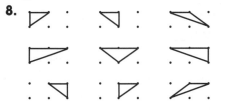

Since there are 9 ways for using the top row as base,
$9 \times 2 = 18$
18 triangles can be drawn.

Page 186

9.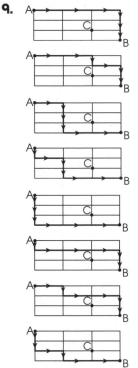

The ants can reach point B in 8 ways.

Page 187

10. 1 stamp: 20¢
50¢
$1

2 stamps: 20¢ + 50¢ = 70¢
20¢ + $1 = $1.20
50¢ + $1 = $1.50

3 stamps: 20¢ + 50¢ + $1 = $1.70

He can make 7 different postage amounts with these stamps.

Page 188

11.   W A T E R   W A T E R   W A T E R

W A T E R   W A T E R   W A T E R

The word "WATER" can be formed in 6 ways.

Page 189

12.

No. of $1 bills	No. of $2 bills	No. of $5 bills	Total value
7	0	0	$7
5	1	0	$7
3	2	0	$7
1	3	0	$7
0	1	1	$7
2	0	1	$7

Leonard can make up a total value of $7 in 6 possible ways.

Page 190

13.

1 AI	1BI	1CI
1AII	1BII	1CII
1AIII	1BIII	1CIII
2AI	2BI	2CI
2AII	2BII	2CII
2AIII	2BIII	2CIII

He can have 18 different combinations.

Page 191

14. All the possible results for the colors of balls he will draw out from the bag are shown below.

RRR   RRW   WWR   GGW   RWG
WWW   RRG   WWG   GGR
GGG

R = Red   W = White   G = Green

Chapter 12 Practice

Page 195

1.

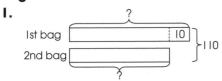

110 – 10 = 100
100 ÷ 2 = 50
50 + 10 = 60
There are 60 beads in one bag and 50 beads in another bag.

Page 196

2.

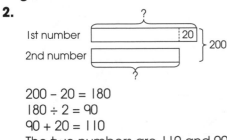

200 – 20 = 180
180 ÷ 2 = 90
90 + 20 = 110
The two numbers are 110 and 90.

Page 197

3.

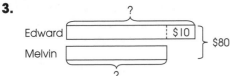

$80 – $10 = $70
$70 ÷ 2 = $35
$35 + $10 = $45
Melvin has $35 and Edward has $45.

Page 198

4. Alison $20
Anna $20 $20 $20 $20
?

4 × $20 = $80
Anna has $80.

Page 199

5.

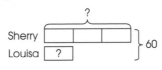

60 ÷ 4 = 15
15 × 3 = 45
Louisa has 15 marbles and Sherry has 45 marbles.

Page 200

6.

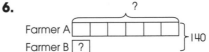

140 ÷ 7 = 20
Farmer A has 120 chickens and Farmer B has 20 chickens.

Page 201

7.

57 – 3 – 6 = 48
48 ÷ 3 = 16
Pears = 16 + 3 = 19
Peaches = 16
Apples = 16 + 6 = 22

Pears [3]
Peaches
Apples [6]
57

There are 19 pears, 16 peaches and 22 apples.

Page 202

8.

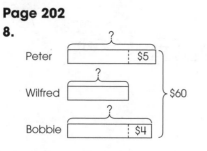

$60 - $5 - $4 = $51
$51 ÷ 3 = $17
$17 + $5 = $22
$17 + $4 = $21
Peter has $22, Wilfred has $17 and Bobbie has $21.

Page 203

9.

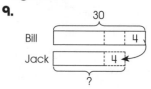

30 - 4 = 26
26 - 4 = 22
Jack has 22 storybooks at first.

Page 204

10.

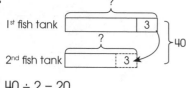

40 ÷ 2 = 20
20 + 3 = 23
20 - 3 = 17
The first fish tank has 23 fish and the second fish tank has 17 fish at first.

Page 205

11.

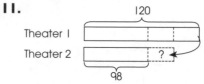

120 - 98 = 22
22 ÷ 2 = 11
Theater 1 = 120 - 11 = 109
Theater 2 = 98 + 11 = 109
11 spectators must move from theater 1 to theater 2 so that both theaters have the same number of audience members.

Page 206

12. 42 + 34 + 14 = 90
90 ÷ 3 = 30

42 - 30 = 12
34 - 30 = 4
12 students from school bus A and 4 students from school bus B must move over to school bus C.

Page 207

13. $12 + 19 + 11 = 42$

$42 \div 3 = 14$

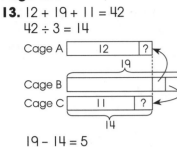

$19 - 14 = 5$

$14 - 11 = 3$

$14 - 12 = 2$

Alan should move 2 parrots from cage B to cage A and 3 parrots from cage B to cage C.

Page 208

14.

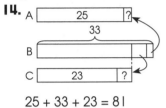

$25 + 33 + 23 = 81$

$81 \div 3 = 27$

$27 - 25 = 2$

$27 - 23 = 4$

2 and 4 oranges from basket B must be transferred to baskets A and C respectively.

Page 209

15. First [diagram: 2 | 5 } 40]
Second [? | 5]

$40 - 2 = 38$

$38 \div 2 = 19$

$19 - 5 = 14$

There are 14 eggs in the second basket at first.

Page 210

16.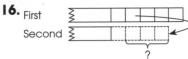

First
Second
?

$4 - 1 = 3$

The second branch would have 3 more sparrows.

978-1-62399-072-5
Singapore Math Challenge

Chapter 13 Practice

Page 214

1. **(a)**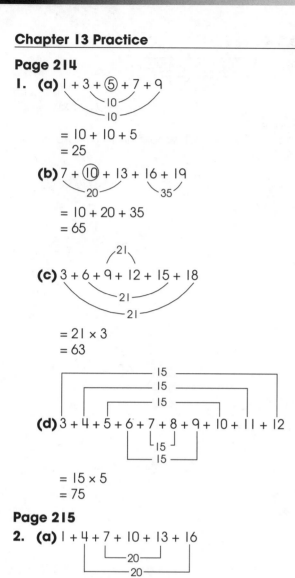

$1 + 3 + ⑤ + 7 + 9$

$= 10 + 10 + 5$

$= 25$

(b) $7 + ⑩ + 13 + 16 + 19$

$= 10 + 20 + 35$

$= 65$

(c) $3 + 6 + 9 + 12 + 15 + 18$

$= 21 \times 3$

$= 63$

(d) $3 + 4 + 5 + 6 + 7 + 8 + 9 + 10 + 11 + 12$

$= 15 \times 5$

$= 75$

Page 215

2. **(a)** $1 + 4 + 7 + 10 + 13 + 16$

$= 1 + 10 + 20 + 20$

$= 51$

(b) $2 + 3 + 4 + 5 + 6 + ⑦ + 8 + 9 + 10 + 11 + 12$

There are 5 pairs of 14 and a remaining 7.

$= 5 \times 14 + 7$

$= 70 + 7$

$= 77$

(c) $10 + 20 + 30 + 40 + 50$

$= 50 \times 3$

$= 150$

(d) $1 + 2 + 3 + 4 + 5 + 6 + 7 + 8 + 9 + 10 + 11 +$
$12 + 13 + 14 + 15 + 16 + 17 + 18 + 19 + 20$

There are 10 pairs of 21.

$= 10 \times 21$

$= 210$

Page 216

3. $24 \div 3 = 8$ or $24 = 8 + 8 + 8$

8	8	8
↓	↓	↓
– 1		+ 1
7	8	9

The three numbers are 7, 8 and 9.

Page 217

4. $50 \div 5 = 10$

10	10	10	10	10
↓	↓	↓	↓	↓
– 2	– 1		+ 1	+ 2
8	9	10	11	12

The five numbers are 8, 9, 10, 11 and 12.

Page 218

5. $54 \div 9 = 6$

6	6	6	6	6	6	6	6	6
↓	↓	↓	↓	↓	↓	↓	↓	↓
–4	–3	–2	–1		+1	+2	+3	+4
2	3	4	5	6	7	8	9	10

The nine numbers are 2, 3, 4, 5, 6, 7, 8, 9 and 10.

Page 219

6. $63 \div 7 = 9$

The seven numbers are 6, 7, 8, 9, 10, 11 and 12.

Page 220

7. (a) $20 + 30 + 40 + \boxed{50} + 60 + 70 + 80$

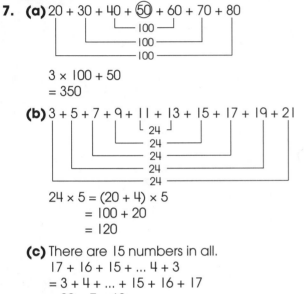

$3 \times 100 + 50$
$= 350$

(b) $3 + 5 + 7 + 9 + 11 + 13 + 15 + 17 + 19 + 21$

$24 \times 5 = (20 + 4) \times 5$
$\quad\quad\quad\; = 100 + 20$
$\quad\quad\quad\; = 120$

(c) There are 15 numbers in all.
$17 + 16 + 15 + ... \; 4 + 3$
$= 3 + 4 + ... + 15 + 16 + 17$
$= 20 \times 7 + 10$
$= 140 + 10 = 150$

(d) There are 20 numbers in all.
$(30 + 11) \times 10$
$= 41 \times 10 = 410$

Page 221

8.

9	9	9
↓	↓	↓
– 2		+ 2

The three consecutive odd numbers are 7, 9 and 11.

Page 222

9. $45 \div 5 = 9$

9	9	9	9	9
↓	↓	↓	↓	↓
– 4	– 2		+ 2	+ 4

The five odd numbers are 5, 7, 9, 11 and 13.

Page 223

10. $63 \div 7 = 9$

The seven odd numbers are 3, 5, 7, 9, 11, 13 and 15.

Page 224

11. 10, 12, 14, 16, 18, 20, 22, 24, 26, 28
There are 28 seats in the 10th row.

Page 225

12. 4, 7, 10, 13, 16, 19, 22, 25, 28, 31
$35 \times 5 = 175$
There were 175 pages in the storybook.

Page 226

13. (a)

4th   5th

(b) The number of dots in each pattern is 1, 3, 6, 10, 15 and 21 respectively.
$1 + 3 + 6 + 10 + 15 + 21 = 56$
There are 56 dots altogether from the 1st to the 6th pattern.

978-1-62399-072-5
Singapore Math Challenge

Page 227

14. (a)

4th   5th

(b) The number of dots in each pattern is 1, 4, 9, 16, 25, 36 and 49 respectively.

$$1 + 4 + 9 + 16 + 25 + 36 + 49$$

25 + 25 + 40 + 50 = 140

There are 140 dots from the 1st to the 7th pattern.

Page 228

15. $56 \div 7 = 8$

8   8   8   8   8   8   8

↓   ↓   ↓   ↓   ↓   ↓   ↓

−6 −4 −2   +2 +4 +6

The seven numbers are 2, 4, 6, 8, 10, 12 and 14.

Page 229

16. $64 \div 8 = 8$

8   8   8   8   8   8   8   8

↓   ↓   ↓   ↓   ↓   ↓   ↓   ↓

−7 −5 −3 −1 +1 +3 +5 +7

The eight numbers are 1, 3, 5, 7, 9, 11, 13 and 15.

Page 230

17. $40 \div 4 = 10$

10 10 10 10

↓   ↓   ↓   ↓

−3 −1 +1 +3

The four numbers are 7, 9, 11 and 13.

Page 231

18. $40 \div 5 = 8$

8   8   8   8   8

↓   ↓   ↓   ↓   ↓

−4 −2   +2 +4

The five numbers are 4, 6, 8, 10 and 12.

Chapter 14 Practice

Page 232

1. (a)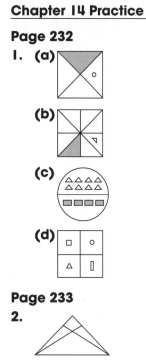

(b)

(c)

(d)

Page 233

2.

Page 234

3.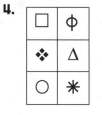

Page 235

4.

Page 236

5.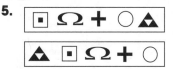

Page 237

6.

7.

Page 238

8.

Page 239

9.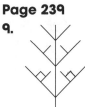

978-1-62399-072-5
Singapore Math Challenge

Page 240

10.

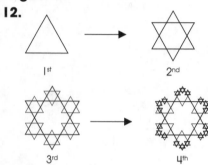

Page 241

11. Figure D is not symmetrical.

Page 242

12.

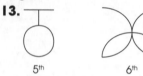

Page 243

13.

Each figure is made up of a number and its mirror image.

Page 244

14.

It is a mirror image of number 6.

978-1-62399-072-5
Singapore Math Challenge

Chapter 15 Practice

Page 245

1. $35 \div 5 = 7$

```
  7      7      7      7      7
  ↓      ↓      ↓      ↓      ↓
 – 4    – 2           + 2    + 4
  3      5      7      9     11
```

There are 3, 5, 7, 9 and 11 marbles in the respective boxes.

Page 246

2. $25 + $5 + $20 = $50

$8 + $12 + $20 + $10 = $50

He can buy 4 items at the most.

Page 247

3. Numbers 1 to 9 = 1

Numbers 10 to 19 = 11

Numbers 20 to 29 = 1

Numbers 30 to 39 = 1

Numbers 40 to 49 = 1

Total = 15

There are 15 "1s" from numbers 1 to 50.

Page 248

4. One of the adventurers had to stay on the rubber raft.

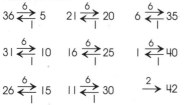

17 trips must be made in order to ferry all adventurers across the river.

Page 249

5. Step 1: Split the 9 coins into 3, 3, 3.

Step 2: Weigh any 2 groups.

If it is balanced, the fake coin is in third group.

If not, the fake coin is in the lighter group.

Step 3: Split the group containing the fake coin into 1, 1, 1.

Step 4: Weigh any 2 of them.

If it is balanced, the fake coin is the one that is not weighed.

If not, the fake coin would be the lighter one.

Page 250

6.

Key	A	B	C	D	E	F
No. of failed attempts	5	4	3	2	1	0

$5 + 4 + 3 + 2 + 1 + 0 = 15$

15 attempts must be made at the most to find the right key to each padlock.

Page 251

7.

I can get 7 slices of pizza at the most.

Page 252

8. $35 = 17 + 18$

The two facing page numbers that Jaclyn is reading are pages 17 and 18.

Page 253

9. $11 \times 12 = 132$

The two facing page numbers that Bryan is reading are pages 11 and 12.

Page 254

10. $11 + 12 + 1 + 2 = 26$
$10 + 9 + 3 + 4 = 26$
$8 + 7 + 6 + 5 = 26$

Page 255

11.

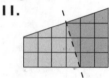

Page 256

12. $12 + 1 = 11 + 2$
$= 10 + 3 = 9 + 4$
$= 8 + 5 = 7 + 6$
$= 13$

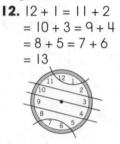

Page 257

13.

Page 258

14. (a)

(b)

(c)

(d)

The figures in (a), (b) and (d) can be formed by the L-shaped tiles.

Page 259

15. $4 + 4 + 2 + 2 = 12$

```
o   o   o   o
o           o
o           o
o   o   o   o
```

Page 260

16.

7	2	9
8	6	4
3	10	5

Page 261

17.

7	12	5
6	8	10
11	4	9

978-1-62399-072-5
Singapore Math Challenge

Chapter 16 Practice

Page 266

1.
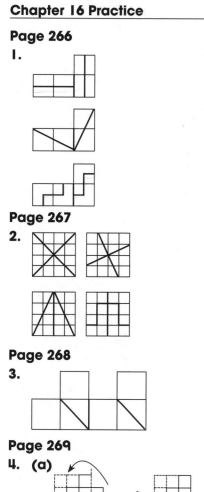

Page 267

2.

Page 268

3.

Page 269

4. (a)

(b)

Page 270

5.
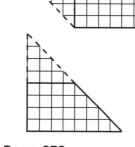

Page 271

6.
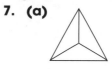

Page 272

7. (a)

(b)

(c)

978-1-62399-072-5
Singapore Math Challenge

Page 273

8.

Page 274

9.

Page 275

10.

Page 276

11.

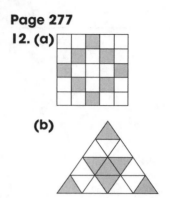

Page 277

12. (a)

(b)

978-1-62399-072-5
Singapore Math Challenge

Chapter 17 Practice

Page 282

1. **(a)** even + odd = odd
   (b) even + odd = odd
   (c) odd − odd = even
   (d) odd + odd = even
   (e) even + even = even
   (f) even − even = even
   (g) odd + odd = even
   (h) odd − odd = even
   (i) even + even = even
   (j) even + odd = odd
   (k) odd − odd = even
   (l) odd − odd = even

Page 283

2. $16 = 1 + 15$
   $16 = 3 + 13$
   $16 = 5 + 11$
   $16 = 7 + 9$
   There are 4 ways to give the marbles away so that each child will have an odd number of marbles.

Page 284

3. $14 = 2 + 12$
   $14 = 4 + 10$
   $14 = 6 + 8$
   There are 3 ways to place the oranges so that each basket contains an even number of oranges.

Page 285

4. 1,   3,   6,   10,   15,   21,   28   ...
    ↑   ↑   ↑   ↑   ↑   ↑   ↑
   odd odd even even odd   odd even
    o o e e o o e e o o e
    o o e̲ e o o e e o o e̲ e
       ↑   ↑
     15th   23rd
   Both the 15th and 23rd terms are even numbers.

Page 286

5. 1,   4,   9,   16,   25,   36   ...
    ↑   ↑   ↑   ↑   ↑   ↑
   odd even odd even odd   even
   The number is even when it is the even term.
   The number is odd when it is the odd term.
   The 10th term is even and the 15th term is odd.

Page 287

6. Odd, as the result of the series is 55.
   There are 5 odd numbers as a result of pairing.
   So, the result of the series is odd.

Page 288

7. $21 \div 3 = 7$
    7   7   7
    ↓   ↓
    − 2   + 2
    5   7   9
   The 3 numbers are 5, 7 and 9.

Page 289

8. $12 = 8 + 2 + 2$
   $12 = 6 + 4 + 2$
   $12 = 4 + 4 + 4$
   There are 3 ways to give the apples so each child will get an even number of apples.

Page 290

9. $1 + 3 + 5 + 7 + 9$
    even + even + odd = odd
    The sum of the first 5 odd numbers is odd.

Page 291

10. $2 + 4 + 6 + 8 + 10$
    even + even + even = even
    The sum of the first 5 even numbers is even.

Page 292

11. 1,   1,   2,   3,   5,   8,   13
    ↑   ↑   ↑   ↑   ↑   ↑
    odd odd even odd odd even
    The pattern is odd, odd, even.
    $16 \div 3 = 5\,R\,1$
    $27 \div 3 = 9\,R\,0$
    The 16th term is odd and the 27th term is even.

Page 293

12. **(a)** 5 such tiles are needed.

(b) 4 such tiles are needed.

(c) 4 such tiles are needed.

Chapter 18 Practice

Page 299

1. ○ ○ ○ ○ ◉ ○ ○ ○
              4   3   2   1

Its position was 4th if we count from the back of the traffic jam.

Page 300

2. ○ ○ ○ ◉ ○ ○ ○ ○ ○ ○ ○

4 + 7 = 11

11 children were in the line.

Page 301

3. 7 + 1 + 7 = 15

There are 15 beads altogether.

Page 302

4. 3 + 1 + 5 = 9

9 members are in the first row of the school choir.

Page 303

5. 15 – 9 = 6

He was 7th from the end of the line.

Page 304

6.

She used 6 clothespins altogether.

Page 305

7. ○ ○ ○ ○ ○ ◉ ○ ○ ○ ◉ ○ ○ ○ ○ ○ ○ ○

6 + 3 + 8 = 17

17 children were in the line.

Page 306

8. 6 + 4 + 6 = 14

14 seats were in the first row.

Page 307

9. ○ ○ ◉ ○ ○ ○ ○ ○ ○ ○ ○ ○ ○ ◉ ○
   ○ ○ ○ ○

18 – 3 – 6 = 9

9 children were between Vanessa and Andrea.

Page 308

10. 90 cm + 10 cm = 100 cm

100 cm = 50 cm + 50 cm

Each plank of wood is 50 cm long.

Page 309

11. 60 cm + 15 cm + 15 cm = 90 cm

90 cm = 45 cm + 45 cm

Each piece of ribbon is 45 cm long.

Page 310

12. 35 + 23 = 58

Yet 10 students took part in both events. So, they have been counted twice.

58 – 10 = 48

48 students took part in the events.

© Singapore Asia Publishers Pte Ltd

978-1-62399-072-5
Singapore Math Challenge